Sexual Difference

Sexual Difference: Masculinity and Psychoanalysis offers a critical exploration of issues of gender in psychoanalysis. It acknowledges and unpacks the complexity of theory and writing in this area, particularly the way sexual difference can only be thought about from a gendered position. As the book is written by a male academic and psychologist, its orientation is towards the way masculinity is expressed in theory and practice, and how this influences the experience and construction of both masculinity and femininity in contemporary culture. In addition, Stephen Frosh describes how psychoanalysis itself can be seen as a system heavily imbued with gender assumptions, and how the form and content of its theories express many of the dilemmas of sexual difference.

Sexual Difference is written in a clear, accessible and also self-reflexive style. It introduces major strands of psychoanalytic theory on sexual difference, particularly those associated with the Kleinian and Lacanian traditions, and includes a detailed exploration of the gender assumptions apparent in some of Freud's work. As well as providing a critical analysis of these psychoanalytical positions, the book also employs them to throw light on such crucial issues for gender politics as sexual violence, language and psychotherapy.

Stephen Frosh is a practising clinical psychologist and an academic psychologist and writer. He has worked for many years in the areas of psychoanalysis, culture and gender, and also with children who have been sexually abused.

Sexual Difference

Masculinity and Psychoanalysis

Stephen Frosh

London and New York

First published 1994
by Routledge
11 New Fetter Lane, London EC4P 4EE

Simultaneously published in the USA and Canada
by Routledge
29 West 35th Street, New York, NY 10001

Typeset in Palatino by
NWL Editorial Services, Langport, Somerset

Printed and bound in Great Britain by
Mackays of Chatham PLC, Chatham, Kent

British Library Cataloguing in Publication Data
A catalogue record for this book is available from the British Library

Library of Congress Cataloging in Publication Data
Frosh, Stephen.
  Sexual difference: masculinity and psychoanalysis/Stephen Frosh.
  p.cm.
  Includes bibliographical references and index.
  1. Masculinity (Psychology) 2. Sex differences (Psychology)
  3. Psychoanalysis. I. Title.
  BF175.5.M37F76 1994   93–5902
  155.3′3–dc20   CIP

ISBN 0–415–06843–6 (hbk)
ISBN 0–415–06844–4 (pbk)

To Joel
and to the memory of Terry Brewer

Contents

Acknowledgements

I would like to thank the following friends and colleagues who have read and commented on the chapters of this book in their various drafts: Charlotte Burck, Anthony Elliott, Joanna Hirst, Laura Marcus, Janet Sayers and Jane Ussher.

An earlier and much shorter version of Chapter 5 appeared in J. Ussher and C. Baker (eds) *Psychological Perspectives on Sexual Problems* (London: Routledge, 1993). A small amount of material in Chapter 1 first appeared in J. Ussher and P. Nicolson (eds) *Gender Issues in Clinical Psychology* (London: Routledge, 1992).

Chapter 1

Finding sexual difference

Sexual difference is a subject which will not go away. The questions it poses are always present, hovering over and in us – how are we the same as one another and how are we different? In what ways are we characteristic of our sex and to what extent can we transgress its boundaries? How can we relate constructively to the problematic categories 'masculine' and 'feminine'? These are categories that seem to determine the perspectives we use to understand ourselves and others, yet they are also lacking in concreteness, making them the source of sweeping generalisations which then always carry profound exceptions. A common formulation of this kind might read, 'Men are . . . Women are . . . But *this particular* man or woman is more like this, not like that, has both sides within.' What can we say or do that might challenge the received wisdom of what is appropriate to being masculine or feminine, whilst also recognising the way people's experiences of themselves are bound up with deeply felt but often implicit notions of what their gender should and does mean?

I have come to writing about sexual difference a long way round, through the route of academic study and clinical psychological practice. In many respects, I have tried to avoid it, as it is so complicated and embarrassing when compared with the realities of my everyday life as a man. But if I am going to write at all, I have to do something with it, going further than my previous dips into the water of psychoanalytic feminism and psychological gender theory (Frosh, 1987a, 1989). Gradually, I have come to see the ubiquity and unavoidability of the questions surrounding sexual difference in my own everyday experience, in my work, and in writing. There seems never to be a moment at which it disappears, there is nothing that can call itself 'gender neutral'; always there is a position or set of experiences which is 'same as mine' and another which is 'other' with which I have to deal, a subject which will not go away.

In 1988, I published, jointly with a female psychiatrist, a book on child sexual abuse (Glaser and Frosh, 1988). For me, the experience of work with sexually abused children was a deeply troubling watershed in my professional life. I was working as a psychologist with children and families, struggling to understand the difficulties for which people were requesting help, but reasonably assured that there was an approach, a set of techniques, or general method of professional practice that could deal with these difficulties, and which in principle I could learn. Child sexual abuse was a new issue, publicly recognised at last because of the efforts of rape crisis and incest survivors' groups, so that for the first time for decades children who said they had been assaulted were beginning to be believed. This alteration of awareness opened floodgates: a surge of people – children and adults – clamouring to be heard and helped; and also a mass of suspicions, claims, and muddles. Professionals working with children were being asked in some way to respond to this clamour, without clear guidelines for action or knowledge of what it might all mean. But amongst the uncertainty produced by this state of affairs, one of the few facts which appeared clear and irrefutable was that when children are sexually abused, they are abused by men.

I worked in a team of men and women, all 'mental health professionals'. We saw these cases and heard new stories we had not heard before. The women became aware of experiences and anxieties of their own. I became aware of being on the other side, of being 'same as' the abusers in their masculinity, of maybe being seen that way by their victims, and consequently of feeling somehow tarnished myself, by association. I kept on thinking, 'Could I do that?', 'Am I one of those?', 'Is there anything I can do to help?' I wrote about this experience and talked about it, informally and formally, aligning myself with a 'progressive' position from which abusiveness could be repudiated but also attempting to recognise its existence in all men, and the effects of this on the work of men who are therapists involved with sexually abused children (Frosh, 1987b, 1988). This created some interest and considerable support amongst male and female professionals, but now I wonder how much of a posture it has been – a verbal acknowledgement of the links between masculinity and abusive-ness that, through the act of acknowledgement, functions to free men from the responsibility for actually *becoming* different. Still, it was worth saying and still needs to be said: we do not strip ourselves of our gender when we work as psychologists or psychotherapists or whatever; but we enact that work in the context of our gender, and vice versa.

When the 1988 book, *Child Sexual Abuse*, came out, there was a furore that gave us our 'fifteen minutes of fame'. Here is the crucial passage, which incidentally is built on in Chapter 5 below. We are discussing possible sources of the empirically established link between masculinity and sexual abuse – that is, the finding that the vast majority of abusers are men.

Traditional 'masculinity' focuses on dominance and independence, an orientation to the world which is active and assertive, which valorises competitiveness and turns its face from intimacy, achieving esteem in the glorification of force. The fear at the heart of this image is of emotion – that which makes us vulnerable and 'womanly'; emotion is dangerous not only because it implies dependence, but also because it is alien, a representative of all that masculinity rejects. This fear of emotion in turn makes sex both over- and under-invested in by men. Sex is one of the few socially acceptable ways in which men can aspire to closeness with others, and as such it becomes the carrier of all the unexpressed desires that men's emotional illiteracy produces. However, this same power of sex to produce emotionality makes it dangerous to men whose identity is built upon the rejection of emotion; sex then becomes split off, limited to the activity of the penis, an act rather than an encounter. It is also a means of taking up a particular place in the world of men: sexual 'conquest' as a symbol of male prowess. The link between such a form of masculinity and sexual abuse is apparent: it is not just present, but *inherent* in a mode of personality organisation that rejects intimacy. Sex as triumph and achievement slides naturally into sex as rejection and degradation of the other.

(Glaser and Frosh, 1988, p. 24)

This passage was taken up energetically in the British press and interpreted to mean that all men are potential abusers – something which was then denied forcefully in the more conservative newspapers. We were accused of 'abusing the family' and of making monstrous assertions against normal men, all the worse because it was clear that we were not extreme feminists, but respectable 'doctors'. In the general context of concern over the Cleveland child abuse controversy in Britain, we were seen as part of a professional conspiracy against traditional values, and in particular against the family.

All this would benefit from some unpicking and analysis, in particular in the light of work on 'moral panics', which seems very relevant to understanding many responses to child abuse (see Levidow, 1989). But I am reviewing this personal history here for other reasons. The passage itself arises out of the experience described above, in which, as a man working in a sphere of male oppression, but working primarily with the victims of that oppression, I had to try to make sense of, and come to terms with, the tensions and discontents that situation produced. The energy of the piece derives from that struggle and also from a wish to repudiate the element of masculinity which I came to regard as abusive – the rejection of intimacy and emotion and the potency of this rejection in the abusing male, whom I would wish to make other than myself. So the broad sweep of the passage, its overstatement and overgeneralisation, is fuelled in part by the desire to be rid of this kind of masculinity, to become something different. I do not think the argument in the passage is wrong; indeed, in this book I try to clarify and develop ideas which can be found in outline within it. But it is not purely explanatory; it is partly a claim that, 'I know this (what masculinity is, what men do) and can own up to it; hence I am different.' In writing of this kind, an alignment is made from within a gendered position; gender is not external and is not escaped, but it is used as fuel for what is said.

The exaggerated response of the media brought home to me another element of relevance for thinking on sexual difference. Whatever they did with the actual material in the book, the journalists understood one thing: that the claim being made (abusiveness is linked with characteristic patterns of sexual socialisation of men) has a place in arguments over gender, sexuality and domination, which are deeply ideological and also central to the social order. The affront to 'common sense' produced by a claim that all men have the possibility of abusive behaviour socialised into them is that this claim challenges the liberal idea that we are all basically reasonable, and that abusive acts are the products of disturbed and criminal personalities. Moreover, it asserts that the taken-for-granted normalities of family life and of childhood sexual and gender socialisation are in fact implicated in a process that institutionalises domination and perpetuates abuse. Challenging these patterns of sexual socialisation is one element in a challenge to the social order which is expressed most cogently in feminism. The added emotional charge of child sexual abuse makes the potency of the challenge that much stronger, but also consequently creates more active resistance in its wake.

For myself, all this has meant that it has been impossible to keep an academic interest in sexual difference separate from professional and personal concerns. The criticism of myself and my co-author were personal, but also professional in the sense that we were taken as representative of a strand of anti-establishment, anti-family welfare work usually seen as the province of leftist social workers rather than psychiatrists and psychologists. But even in this, the stakes were personal: asserting that all men are implicated in the processes leading to sexual abuse makes men feel accused. I have that feeling myself, and find myself working with and against it much of the time.

The therapeutic work with which I have been primarily engaged as a psychologist has been in child and family contexts, in which a sphere defined primarily in 'feminine' terms – family life – is subjected to the scrutiny of a professional world largely inhabited by women, but including a fair sprinkling of 'expert' men. I find myself talking with women and children, and with men when they can be persuaded to come to meetings, about personal concerns and worries which they may have; and I experience myself as positioned as expert, yet also as potentially not understanding what is happening, because I am 'wrongly' gendered, not knowing the women's view. Before introducing the more academic thinking around which much of this book is organised, I want to recognise the effects of this, and to note how my attempts to deal with it practically and theoretically have been marked by an impulse to establish the *value* of difference. This involves an attempt to create a gender identity which has some ambiguity and flexibility (so that it is possible to take up the position of the woman, to understand or empathise), but which is consciously not a denial of difference, thus allowing for the possibility that a man might bring in another point of view. Much of what follows in this book concerns the tension created by this enterprise, simultaneously constructing and denying the fixed categories of masculine and feminine distinctiveness. Here, however, I want to give an example of the processes at work, and to do this I will reproduce and then comment on a section from some previously published material. In this, I try to show how my status as a male therapist intersects with a relatively 'maternal' stance towards 'containing' the distress of the patient (a stance linked in this passage with Bion's (1962) notion of 'reverie'), to construct an alternative set of meanings which might only be available through the challenge presented by gender difference. This material was originally published in a slightly altered form in a book on *Gender Issues in Clinical Psychology* (edited by Ussher and Nicolson, 1992), to which I was the only male contributor – a situation that created a whole set of affiliations and tensions of its own. It begins with a short case description, which is then discussed in terms of its gender elements.

The referral to the child and family clinic was made by Mrs M., on the advice of her child Mary's school. Mary, aged six, was compulsively masturbating, constantly rubbing herself against tables. She used to do this at home but had recently stopped. The rubbing was so severe that Mary made herself sore and had bruises in the genital area. There had been considerable involvement in the family from their health visitor and family doctor, who did not believe that Mary was being sexually abused.

The family consisted of Mr M. (aged 35), Mrs M. (aged 33), who had worked in the same office as her husband but was now at home with the children full time, Mary and three other young children. They were seen by myself and a female psychiatric social worker with whom I had never previously worked.

In the first session, Mrs M. was very dominant. Mr M. was quiet and took no initiative with respect to the children, although when his wife told him to do something he was quite effective. Mrs M. was very aggressive towards us – an aggression symbolised by her bringing her knitting to the session, which coincided with the anniversary of the French revolution. She confronted us, demanding explanations for her child's behaviour, but she also made fun of us – for instance saying about me, 'he just sits there and takes it all in'. She described how Mary used to masturbate at home but stopped when she was firm with her and shouted at her. Mrs M. portrayed her husband in angry and derogatory terms, particularly because of his unavailability to the children or her. She said that he spends his time working in the garden shed, leaving her to do everything in the house. He is quiet, she talks. Mary was described as reasonably assertive at home, but she was noticeably passive and frightened in the session, while her siblings took easy control of the room. Mrs M. told us that she interceded for Mary at home, because her sister is always taking away her things or hurting her and there is a great deal of competitiveness between them.

The second session began in the same way. Mrs M. told us that she had been appalled that we had discussed Mary in front of her – she claimed that the school and the health visitor were equally critical of us. She doubted our ability to do anything and had brought her knitting with her again so as not to waste the time. Mr M. sat quietly, answering questions asked of him but saying little else. My colleague and I were acutely conscious of Mrs M.'s sardonic glances at us. We felt antagonistic towards her, wondering how the children could manage to survive – it was not surprising, we thought, that Mary was in such a state. Her masturbation was the same as ever, almost constant at school. Mrs M. got annoyed when we asked if she ever went into school, saying that the other mothers did, but how could she when she had young children to look after at home? She challenged my silence, asking if I had anything to offer her at all. I responded with a very direct intervention, developing and verbalising a hypothesis there and then, suggesting that Mary found school harder than people realise, that she knew her mother could not come in to help her as she does at home unless something really extreme happens, and that she had realised that her constant rubbing was just such an extreme thing. Mrs M. suddenly began to listen, seeming very engaged in what was being said. We left the family to think about this idea, also asking Mr M. to take more control over the children.

This last section of the session proved to be a turning point in our work with the family: subsequently Mrs M., whilst still provocative and demeaning of her husband, worked hard with us to understand and help her child. Indeed, following one low-key visit by us to the school, Mary's compulsive rubbing ceased with no particular intervention, and the focus of the sessions shifted to Mrs M.'s anger at the lack of support she felt herself to be receiving from her husband – in particular, his lack of emotional responsiveness.

There are obviously a number of reasons why the changes in this family may have occurred, some at least of which might have been located outside therapy, for instance in changes in the schoolteacher's perception of Mary. Moreover, this was by no means a perfect piece of family therapy, nor does it have perfectly anti-sexist credentials. Perhaps characteristically for a male therapist, my focus was not on the male patient; indeed, it may have been that the relative insignificance of my female colleague in this session was due to my usurpation of her isometry with Mrs M. – we both competed for the ear of the woman. Change came about, but as usual through the mother; the opportunity to challenge the father's secure unavailability to his wife and children was left mainly unrecognised. A few suggestions, but not too much conflict or pain. Or maybe there is another, partially contradictory source to this overdetermined sequence: by not challenging the male, by focusing on changes in the woman, we men are in a happy identificatory collusion. After all, structuralists claim the woman to be the object of exchange between men. Also, of course, my potency as therapist has its competitive edge with my colleague/rival: when the male takes over, the professional voice is heard. We all wait to see what rabbit will be pulled out of his hat.

But I want, or need, to find something positive in this by focusing on just one element in the family-therapist relationship, the meaning of the therapy for Mrs M. There appeared to be a 'transformational moment' in the second session when, riled by Mrs M.'s challenge, I managed to offer something that both surprised and engaged her. Some of it may have had to do with the content of the 'hypothesis' about Mary's behaviour, which seemed to make sense to Mrs M. But I think something else happened too. With her husband, the pattern was for his withdrawal to be reinforced by her aggressive attacks – her withering remarks, experienced by him as emasculating. Alongside this dynamic, Mrs M. actually felt terrible about what Mary was doing, believing that it indicated a severe failure in parenting on her own part, for after all she was charged with – and had taken on for herself – complete responsibility for all that happened with her children. In addition, she felt strongly identified with Mary, seeing Mary's personality as just like her own. I think that this combination of factors, plus other elements in Mrs M.'s history, led her to feel quite desperate about herself, overwhelmed both by anger and by an intolerable sense that Mary, by damaging herself, was actually damaging her. My response, in most respects quite accidentally (or unconsciously?), broke into this vicious cycle. First, the content of it was not blaming of her. More importantly, however, its context was as a response to Mrs M.'s challenge; it was animated by my sense of being disturbed by her, as a man and a therapist and a male therapist, but it was not really an aggressive assault. I had neither withdrawn nor exploded, the two categories of masculine response in Mrs M.'s fantasy and in the cultural order as a whole; instead, I had accidentally, unconsciously cued into her own emotional tone – desperation and rage rather than violence – and made something of it.

I was not particularly full of reverie that day, but perhaps just enough to register the message underneath the words. Moreover, I think it was important that it was I rather than my female co-worker who hit upon the response. The sexual challenge in Mrs M.'s behaviour was very strong, as it was too in her daughter's behaviour – which may have been an unconscious echo of Mrs M.'s sense of the destructiveness of her own sexuality. In any event, my maleness was significant to her, both in traditional transferential ways and as a specific marker of difference. I was not identified with her, not 'same' like her daughter, so my acknowledgement of her emotional state came from somewhere other than her, breaking into her consciousness to turn things around. My difference from her made my apparent understanding of, and sympathy for, her that much more unexpected and therefore powerful: that someone so 'other' could recognise her perhaps meant that the recognition was experienced as more real, less capable of being reduced to collusion or pity. My masculinity was a challenge to her, which is why she challenged me: she had to triumph. But when we escaped this dance, this symmetry, it was a difference that helped her renew herself.

(Adapted from Frosh, 1992a, pp. 164–7)

Reading this material through now, a number of issues stand out for consideration. Some of the problems with the clinical work are actually taken up in the commentary which immediately follows it, particularly in relation to the treatment of my female co-therapist (who is given no part to play at all in the whole story) and in the neglect of the father – seen as a characteristic failing of male therapists, who tend not to address the issues of collusion with, or challenge of, male patients if there is a woman also available with whom to work. To some extent, of course, this is a self-protective strategy: by recognising the problems with the work, I avoid being criticised – a common strategy for men writing in the general arena of anti-sexist practice.

More important than this, however, is the tone and content of the passages which follow, where the task I have set myself is to articulate the reasons for the apparently powerful effect of my intervention with Mrs M., and to understand these in gendered terms. The case being made is for the significance of ownership of gender coupled with a transgression of gender expectations. On the one hand, my masculinity serves as a challenge to Mrs M, and her femininity as a challenge to me; they sexualise proceedings in a way which might have been much less apparent in a same-sex coupling. On the other hand, I claim to take the trouble with her not to be aggressive or withdrawn, but to try to make sense. To a considerable degree I still stand by this analysis, but re-reading the passage makes me very aware of the self-justificatory knowingness of its tone. Uncomfortable in and with the work, uncertain as to whether I have described a conventional employment of male power or a genuinely enabling transgression of gender expectations, I take on an explanatory tone and the writing becomes forced. The case becomes, 'difference is more powerful than sameness, so feminist claims for the power of female solidarity are too limited, a form of narcissism'. Hence the closing section of the chapter from which the case material is drawn, which runs as follows:

> Somewhere in this material lies a starting-point for a revaluation of the masculine position in psychological therapy. Its drawbacks have been described in detail earlier: attempts at control, vicarious emotionality, power-manipulation and exploitation of the other in the service of the self. But the productive side of it is the introduction of difference, the realisation that therapy is not just about self-confirmation but is also about challenge. In work with women, acceptance of the other and refusal of mastery intersects with the confrontation implicit in speaking from the position of otherness – encouraging an expectation of difference but also subverting its presumed content. In work with men, the 'mothering' stance of empathic reverie combines with the power of apparent sameness to confuse the accepted categories of what is appropriate to masculine speech and modes of inter-relationship. In both instances, there is the potential for psychological therapy to be a creative struggle, in which the ability of the therapist to be at one with the other also allows articulation of critical challenges and a breaking out from the circle of sameness into which gender so often forces us. All of this is about sexual difference after all, and making a difference is what therapists are supposed to be trying to do.
>
> (Frosh, 1992a, p. 169)

'Difference' becomes validated for its own sake, and the categories of sexual difference – masculine, feminine – are to a considerable degree re-established, despite my attempt to criticise and deconstruct them. The specific strategic importance of this is as a response to my own doubts about my contribution to therapeutic work – about what I am doing being 'expert' to this woman's status as 'client'. As mentioned above, I was the only male contributor to the book in which that chapter appeared, and it now seems clear to me that I felt it to be necessary to construct an argument that would establish the significance of what I might say from that perspective – that might claim a place for the man.

This leaves me with some very uneasy feelings. I have to work in the context of gender all the time, and know that I cannot deny the existence of difference – it is apparent constantly; sexual difference is a subject which will not go away. But if I try to make a space for my masculinity in my work, particularly in my therapeutic work, I risk reproducing oppositions that bolster conventional divisions and assumptions rather than 'deconstructing' them and creating a more fluid space in which masculinity and femininity can merge. Put differently, I am aware of dangers involved in assuming that 'masculinity' and 'femininity' are fixed entities; yet when, partly in response to feminism, I explore the specific impact of working with a 'masculine' perspective I reassert their concreteness and produce yet more oppositions along conventional lines. How can the material presence of sexual difference be recognised without creating conditions under which that difference becomes an absolute state of affairs?

TOWARDS PSYCHOANALYSIS

This book is dedicated to the struggle to write as a man about sexual difference; that is, to find a way of writing from the subjective position of 'masculinity' and yet emerge into a space which unsettles that position and its assumed complementarity with 'femininity'. It will already be clear what a tall order this is, and how contradictory. In order to write 'as a man', that category of perception and being which is defined as 'masculine' has in some way to be held still, so that experience can be constructed around it – a masculine view on this, that and the other. Indeed, in order to theorise about the possibility of *transgressing* gender assumptions, some standing has to be given to the relative stability of the categories themselves – only if 'masculinity' and 'femininity' exist and have power can the subversive process of undermining or muddling them have meaning. Part of the deconstructive process is precisely the revelation that masculinity and femininity are *constructed* categories, without any establishable essence, so transgressing them is both possible and obvious, anyone's liberty. But it is clear from the clinical example given above, and from millions of others, that escaping these 'constructed' categories is no easy task.

Cixous articulates a version of this argument to which I frequently return, as it conveys both a passionate conviction that sexual difference is a culturally constructed phenomenon, and an awareness of the difficulty involved in appreciating the full implications of this conviction.

> There is 'destiny' no more than there is 'nature' or 'essence' as such. Rather, there are living structures that are caught and sometimes rigidly set within historico-cultural limits so mixed up with the scene of History that for a long time it has been impossible (and it is still very difficult) to think or even imagine an 'elsewhere'.
>
> (Cixous, 1975, p. 83)

The social constructionist argument is that femininity and masculinity are organised formulations into which are inserted the potentially myriad ways of experiencing the world. They are constructions which are built around anatomical difference, signifying only because they are granted significance in the context of the particular power relationships that constitute, and historically have constituted, our social environment. Masculinity and femininity are subjective positions, central to our concepts of self because we live in a world divided along gendered lines, but in principle they are just positions, ways of seeing and speaking about what we see. In practice, however, they become fixed: the realities of power bolster the reduction from subjective to objective, from psychological to physical, from gender (a psychological and behavioural state) to sex (a chromosomal and anatomical one). It becomes impossible to *see* them as constructs, and so they become absolutes. In the Lacanian terms to be explored more fully later, the 'phallus' is taken to be the emblem of power and then identified with the male penis. But neither the taking nor the identifying can be left unquestioned – neither the assumption that there is one model of power nor the claim that this model is by its very nature male; some other regulation of sexual difference and subjectivity might be theorised, if only we can force ourselves to 'imagine an "elsewhere" '.

In this area of debate as in others, there is a liking for clear and simple dichotomies which become affiliated to the equally simple polarity of masculine versus feminine. Hard–soft, tight–loose, rigid–pliable, dry–fluid, objective–subjective; these oppositions have become so 'real', so embedded in all our assumptions, that they can be found everywhere, in psychotherapy no less than in other engagements of people with one another. It takes a great effort of mind to hold onto the idea that they are *constructed*, not naturally given, oppositions. What has come to be called 'masculinist' ideology plays on the fact that living with an awareness of the potential fluidity of sexual difference is an extremely difficult task, and goes on to reify masculinity and femininity, making what are essentially social readings of the significance of anatomical difference into concrete things with specific attributes, all the more readily then to disparage the feminised pole. Moreover, this ideological action can be seen not only in the content of the individual terms of the polarity 'masculine versus feminine', but also in the enthusiasm with which these terms are opposed. That is, it is the very act of opposing masculine to feminine – of constituting the one by means of contrast with the other – that ensures the continuation of their dichotomous relationship and makes it possible for domination to occur.

How can one oppose this procedure whilst also adequately recognising the power of gender categories to define the boundaries of people's lives? More specifically in this psychological context, how can one promote ideas stressing the relative arbitrariness of gender divisions whilst also acknowledging that most people experience their 'masculinity' or 'femininity' as something very central to their subjective experience of their identity? Trying to come to terms with the discomfort that this difficulty produces, I return again and again to psychoanalysis. There are obvious problems with this: the misogynistic components of psychoanalytic theory and practice have been well documented, and some of these will be looked at again in this book. No theory can escape such scrutiny, let alone one in which controversial notions such as 'castration complex' and 'penis envy' are given such centrality. Looked at in this light, it is not surprising that psychoanalysis has been often seen more as part of the problem of the continuing domination of patriarchy and misogyny than as part of the solution to it. But what psychoanalysis does offer, in theory and in therapeutic practice, is an approach to subjectivity which is in large part *founded* on the ambiguities of gender – the tension induced by the apparent oppositions of masculinity and femininity, of desire and otherness. From the time of its inception to the present day, sexual difference has been one of the dominant issues in theoretical work in psychoanalysis, and one of the main strands of opposition fuelling disputes between alternative psychoanalytic schools, as well as criticism of psychoanalysis as a whole. One case I will be trying to make in this book is that psychoanalysis at its very core is *about* sexual difference; it is constituted in it and through it, acting it out as it tries to pronounce upon it. From Freud's early work with mainly female hysterical patients, to Lacan's pronouncements on feminine sexuality and the response to this from psychoanalytic feminists (and feminist psychoanalysts), psychoanalysis has been immersed in a tense crossing-over between masculine and feminine, usually with the former theorising the other – but not always. Based though it is on assumptions concerning the significance of sexuality in human existence, psycho-analysis has never fully coped with the way in which sexual difference comes into play, and the uncertainty that is brought about by this situation shows all the time.

These ambiguities make psychoanalytic theory fertile ground for exploring the problem of what it means to construct a masculine perspective on sexual difference that subverts the categories of difference at the same time as employing them. Psychoanalysis is both embroiled in patriarchal conceptions of sexual difference and offers some conceptual and practical tools for examining and disturbing those conceptions. It is genuinely part of the solution as well as part of the problem. Indeed, an argument which I shall develop particularly in Chapter 3, when considering Freud's self-presentation in *The Interpretation of Dreams*, is that the tension between working within established gender categories and attempting to transcend or transgress them is one from which much of the creativity of psychoanalysis arises. But it still leaves problematic the issue of how to employ psychoanalysis in its deconstructive, liberatory function, without becoming immersed in its normativeness; an exact parallel to the question posed earlier of how to talk or write 'from' a gendered position without reinforcing traditional gender oppositions.

PSYCHOANALYSING SEXUAL DIFFERENCE

One distinctive characteristic of psychoanalysis is its focus on subjectivity, on the articulation of what, for want of a better term, can be called the 'inner world'. This suggests that an examination of the extent to which psychoanalysis offers a plausible account of the 'inner experience' of being positioned as masculine or feminine would be a helpful way to proceed, if possible separating this out both from biological considerations and from the specific operations of social forces. But even this apparently innocent starting point is problematic. For one thing, the masculine orientation of psychoanalytic theory itself is something often left untheorised, although awareness of it is recognisable in some of the debates around psycho-analytic feminism stemming from the first psychoanalytic period as well as more recent times (see Mitchell, 1974; Sayers, 1991), and it is self-consciously played upon in some Lacanian work. In general, however, many masculinist assumptions are endemic to psychoanalytic theory itself, thus vitiating any claim it may have to give a gender-free account of sexual difference – notions such as the importance of rational control over 'irrational' desire, the centrality of a paternal law-giving, culture-creating function in individual and social development, or even the therapeutic necessity of the translation of feelings into speech, of the body into words. All of these assumptions are linked to a traditional masculine–feminine opposition in which stereotypically 'masculine' attributes are given precedence. As will be seen at various points of this book, many of these assumptions have been challenged by workers within a generally psychoanalytic tradition, but it is still the case that they are ubiquitous enough to make it impossible simply to use psychoanalysis as a neutral tool for investigating sexual difference. Instead, in each instance where psychoanalytic theory is brought into play, its own gender values have to be uncovered and taken into account.

Another difficulty involved in employing psychoanalysis to give an account of the gendered construction of the inner world is that the distinction 'inner/outer' is itself deconstructed by psychoanalytic reve-lations of the mutual interpenetration of inner and outer space. This takes the form of accounts of how what we see as objective and other is invested in by us and given form by our own unconscious imagery (for example through the processes known as 'projection' and 'projective identification'); and of how what we see as most private to each of us is itself largely constructed through the interminable processes of negotiation of attachment and concern, desire and loss. Psychoanalysis makes the borders permeable and transparent, makes it harder to hold onto a notion of 'subjective' as distinct from 'objective', inside as clearly separable from outside. As such, psychoanalysis itself is a slippery thing: even in the midst of striving towards objectivity, it reveals the subjective urges from which it has arisen – it shows something of the problematic forces of which it is striving to offer an account. Psychoanalytic theory thus evokes experience as much as it explains it, producing a form of knowledge which is more akin to a process of recognition – of finding articulated what is already half-perceived from our own experiences of ourselves, our own dreams and pathologies – than it is to a purely cognitive appropriation of ideas.

There is even an argument that it is impossible to describe psychoanalysis without having been immersed in an analysis oneself. This is not an argument I can accept completely, as it smacks too much of religious conversion or mystical transformation (Gellner, 1992; Frosh, 1992b), but it has something to it. Because psychoanalysis deals with the expression of the irrational codes of unconscious knowledge, it cannot be reduced to the ownership of an idea – to nothing more than a formal logic (although it has to have logic, too). Moreover, psychoanalytic knowledge is a form of activity, an action: it is 'performative' in the sense that it has effects outside the cognitive domain. This is most clearly seen in the employment of psychoanalysis as a mode of therapy, an activity that is directed at making an impact on people and bringing about some form of change. More generally, psychoanalytic theory is reflexive in the sense that it applies to the theoriser and the 'consumer' of the theory in a very direct way, so that if it is taken to heart it might affect the way in which people see themselves and their lives. On a broader level still, psychoanalysis has influenced twentieth-century western culture so much that it is extremely difficult to think oneself into a position in which psychoanalytic notions about personality and development do not operate; our culture would look quite different without them. Consequently, to engage with psychoanalytic understanding one has to explore its personal as well as its scientific resonance; restricting it to cognition, to intellect, removes its most radical part.

This produces a set of problems concerning the possibility of using psychoanalysis theoretically at all. Because psychoanalysis makes all forms of presentation and representation symptomatic, even the most 'academic' writing becomes indicative of certain personal stances – revealing what is being avoided as much as what is being said. If I write about sexual difference in a way devoid of any personal reference, it might suggest a number of things about me – for example, that I use intellectual activity as a means of attempting to master problematic areas in my life, or that I split private from public material so as to appear to deal with threatening issues without actually changing anything. Socially and institutionally, academic writing about emotive topics can be a way of managing and silencing the dangerous elements in those topics, as well as subduing pressure for change; in the context of sexual difference, this might be thought of as a traditional masculine response to feminist criticism. On the other hand, evocative, emotional writing is not something which comes easily in an academic context, precisely because of the focus on rational debate. The 'maleness' of this focus is something which has been much discussed and which is real enough as a representation of the dominant academic traditions of argument and competition, of logic employed as a weapon with which to master the opponent and make one's own name. When academic men do make a self-conscious effort to write differently, more personally and emotionally – to do something approximating to what some feminists call 'writing the body' – it does not often work, frequently coming across as apology ('I am sorry I am not a woman') or patronising ('I am unlike other men, I know what feelings are'). Very often, too, it is boring writing, the life knocked out of it, neither fish nor fowl.

In this book, I have decided to work at this problem of language by examining the tone and structure of the psychoanalytic theories which I employ, as well as their content. If psychoanalysts are right and mode of expression is indicative of underlying feelings, this will be true too of the theories which they themselves produce. Of course, there is a potentially infinite regress here, in that my own writing is not so polished that it can obscure my feelings about the material, and my unresolved difficulties with it. But that is part of the point: this book is part of my attempt to find a way to acknowledge and also transgress received gender categories, and the difficulties and obscurities of that endeavour will be visible within it. What I am attempting to do is both to apply and to examine some psychoanalytic approaches to sexual difference; doing both those things at the same time is bound to create some fractures through which my own struggles around gender and identity will show.

In this chapter, I have tried to describe how the motivation for this book arises in part (and only in part because, following Freud, there are always numerous sources of motivation for anything) from the unsettling impact of sexual difference on my professional practice and on my writing. Originally, the book was intended to be 'about masculinity', but I found myself unable to write about masculinity without questions concerning psychoanalysis' exploration of femininity creeping in. Consequently, the book has come to be 'about' sexual difference from the perspective of masculinity; that is, it is a quite personal, and therefore male, exploration of what psychoanalysis has to say about sexual difference, and conversely of how sexual difference can be found within psychoanalytic theory itself.

As a manifestation of this personal perspective, the topics which I focus on in the book have a masculine bias. Chapter 2 looks at the way psychoanalytic theory often plays out its genderedness in its form and language, and in the process compares the two main strands of work drawn upon in the book – those derived from Melanie Klein and Jacques Lacan. Very crudely speaking, these strands of work reveal, respectively, an emphasis on maternity and on paternity that in each case has far-reaching implications for the theory as a whole, and for the account of sexual difference which is produced by it. Although the Lacanian/ paternal strand predominates in this book, again presumably as a function of my masculine starting point, Kleinianism offers a very significant critical dimension to which I frequently return.

Psychoanalysis' origins lie with Freud, and in Freud's work there is a constant refrain over the difficulty of moving from the masculine position to an understanding of femininity. In Chapter 3, I take the most explicitly autobiographical of Freud's major writings, *The Interpretation of Dreams*, which can perhaps be thought of as the founding script of psychoanalysis, and examine the way in which tensions and ambiguities over sexual difference can be found in the text as a whole, and in particular in the dreams of his own which Freud reports. Analysis of *The Interpretation of Dreams* shows both the ubiquity of sexual difference in personal psychology – Freud's as much as that of anyone else – and how, through this personal dimension, it is there at the origin of psychoanalysis itself.

The psychoanalyst who has had the most marked influence on thinking on sexual difference in recent times is Jacques Lacan, who of course claimed to be perpetrating a 'return to Freud' and who certainly attempted to recreate the spirit of the early gender debates. In Chapter 4, I examine in detail a paper which is often taken as Lacan's position statement on his favourite concept, 'The Meaning of the Phallus'. This paper is explicitly concerned with sexual difference, and it deals with that concern not just in its content (the nature and function of the phallus in masculine and feminine psychology), but in its structure and particularly its style. It is only through reading the paper at both levels – content and form – that the power of Lacan's analysis can be seen, as well as its diversions and problems. Indeed, it becomes apparent that the issue of power, of 'mastery', is what is most at stake.

The questions of domination and phallic mastery (as well as vulnerability) which arise through examination of the Lacan paper lead on to a broader examination of the sources of masculine sexuality, particularly sexual abusiveness. As I have already described in this chapter, this has been an issue with which I have been concerned because of my own professional work, particularly in terms of the emotional and therapeutic fall-out from child sexual abuse. In Chapter 5, I try to make sense of masculine sexual violence by employing both Kleinian and Lacanian frameworks to understand men's sexual socialisation. This chapter is less concerned with a deconstruction of psychoanalysis than with an application of it to a problem of considerable urgency, and one which seems to be near to the core of the tragic elements of sexual difference.

The final chapter of the book takes the argument into a more therapeutic domain. Psychoanalysis functions on the boundaries of what can be understood about personal experience, and its playfulness and tension with regard to sexual difference are one element in this. Chapter 6 begins with the apparent knowingness of the Lacanian account of sexual difference and shows how problematic and uncertain this actually is. Using ideas from a range of post-Lacanian sources, but particularly some Kleinian-influenced work by Julia Kristeva, I try both to unpack the gender assumptions present in some psychoanalytic notions of psychotherapy and to catch some glimpses of a possibly more gender-subversive practice. The chapter then takes this further with a re-examination of some material on identity and marginality to argue a way forward towards the productive transgression of existing gender categories.

This book, then, is both personal and academic; and if the personal elements become swallowed up by, and hidden within, the academic ones, that is perhaps partly an enactment of the dilemmas and inhibitions produced by our current constructions of sexual difference. At some point, maybe it will become possible to find another way of dealing with the same issues; sexual difference is a subject which will not go away.

Chapter 2

Psychoanalysis and sexual difference

A GIFT OF LANGUAGE

Psychoanalytic writing can often be dense and difficult, abstracting concepts to such a degree that they appear to be completely divorced from the clinical and textual contexts in which psychoanalytic practice is actually located. At other times, however, it can be evocative and moving, illuminating by its form and style the ideas and controversies reflected upon in its content. This is true particularly of Freud's own writing, as will be seen in Chapter 3; indeed, Freud's stylistic elegance has played no small part in the dissemination of psychoanalysis generally, and in the continuing fascination which his work holds. But it is more than elegance or linguistic mastery which is at issue here. It is, rather, the extent to which psychoanalytic writing is *alive*; that is, the extent to which it reveals rather than obscures the passion from which it arises. The best psychoanalytic writing, consequently, is not just persuasive science, it is good *literature*, embracing ideas and experiences in ways which are both explanatory and expressive. It is also, in a most important way, 'performative'; that is, it has effects which appear not just in the cognitive sphere (as new ideas) but in the spheres of emotion and experience – it is writing that makes a difference.

The paradigmatic psychoanalytic situation is the clinical one, in which the speech of the analyst is intended to have an impact on the patient, and this impact, or the cumulation of small impacts of this kind, is important. Psychoanalysts know how much more than just telling the truth is involved here, how 'insight' of the psychoanalytic variety depends as much on the emotional and relational context in which the interpretation that produces it is set as on the actual semantic content of the interpretation itself. The words of the analyst become performative when they are attuned to the transference situation that prevails at the time they are uttered, and when they are spoken in the right way, with a structure and form that allows them to be heard and responded to – unconsciously as well as with the intellect. Similarly, psychoanalytic speaking or writing about theory and practice has an impact when it is attuned to the personal and cultural factors that make it important – and when it shows and acknowledges traces of the forces from which it arises. Fortunately for my concerns in this book, much psychoanalytic writing on sexual difference is of this variety. It wears its heart on its sleeve, clearly part of some great debate held in a tense atmosphere, a debate in which issues are alive and significant, in which passion is still present and can be felt. This is why it is both possible and important to think about *how* psychoanalysis discusses sexual difference, as well as *what* it has to say – that is, to engage in a kind of analytic approach to the psychoanalytic material.

As a way of entering into this analytic process, I want to consider one response to the work of a psychoanalyst around whom many transferences cohere, Jacques Lacan. In the area of work on sexual difference, no other psychoanalyst has had as profound an impact in recent times as has he, nor provoked as much controversy and personal malice. Much of this book is a meditation on the productive and constraining impacts of some of Lacan's ideas. But to begin with, I want to consider one very specific response, by an important female academic, to the imagery and purport of Lacan's theory. Here is Felman's (1987) account of what it means to speak analytically, an account placed in the context of her own excited evocation of Lacan:

> Each time the analyst speaks, interprets in the analytic situation, he gives something asked of him. What he gives, however, is not a superior understanding, but a reply. The reply addresses not so much what the patient says (or means), but his call. Being fundamentally a reply to the subject's question, to the force of his address, the interpretive gift is not constative (cognitive) but performative: the gift is not so much a gift of truth, of understanding or of meaning: it is, essentially, a gift of language.
>
> (Felman, 1987, p. 119)

A gift of language: psychoanalysis provides the words to say what has to be said, yet would otherwise remain unspoken. This involves, according to Felman, not just attaching a name to something – diagnosing, for example, the particular complex from which a patient suffers, or, more generally, describing sexual difference in terms that will for ever fix it in one place, so that we all know exactly what it means. What Felman calls 'the interpretive gift' is not of this kind; indeed, analysis dies whenever it has recourse to such techniques. Rather, psychoanalytic speech moves us on when it is capable of listening between the lines of what is said to the call which underlies it, which Felman indicates is a wish for a response from the other. In that very simple and specific sense, psychoanalytic speech is a relationship.

In a passage which is the apparent source of Felman's description, Lacan himself puts the issues like this:

The function of language is not to inform but to evoke. What I seek in speech is the response of the other. What constitutes me as a subject is my question.

(Lacan, 1953, p. 86)

Felman's paragraph is a response to, and gloss on, Lacan's statement – it is the woman's response to this speech of the man. Something important happens here: he speaks, she elaborates; his version is pithy, its sentences short and precise; hers is slower, more expansive. He makes all of language the subject of his utterance, she limits herself to the place of language in psychoanalysis. In addition, Lacan's speech is self-reflexive and tautological: the function of language is 'not to inform but to invoke', so when he says this it also applies to his own utterance and we can ask, 'What is he evoking?', or more specifically, given the end of the quoted statement, 'What is his question?'. Presumably it is something like, 'Can anyone hear me speak?'. Felman, on the other hand, presents a meaningful elaboration of this speech. Her answer to Lacan's question is, 'Yes, I know what you mean, you do make sense after all, and I will explain it and pass it on'. Is this not the woman's traditional role, to make the man feel heard – that all he has to do is speak and she will be there to listen? Moreover, she takes something which is very coded and abrupt, and expands it until it is more graceful and comprehensible, using the more generous language of the gift. Indeed, looked at more closely it can be seen that the content as well as the form of Felman's paragraph is a reply to Lacan: he talks about the subject's question, she describes the analyst's response. She gives the 'gift of language' to Lacan.

Men's speech and women's speech. The man here speaks apparently casually, enigmatically but also forcefully; he knows what the function of language is. The woman writes it out more fully, more carefully, explaining the context in which it applies. But it would be wrong to read Felman's passage as merely subordinated to Lacan's textual authority; her speech is performative as well, not just a gloss or a way of acknowledging a debt to another's ideas. It is more like a gesture of love, a gift of love in which Lacan's speech, self-contradictory and deliberately devoid of precise meaning, is nurtured so that something can be made of it, some new truth made known. Again, this is a gendered act. The man does it quickly, implants the seed; the woman makes it grow. In this apparently neutral academic dialogue, not seeming to be about sexual difference at all, something very conventionally gendered happens between the participants: the man speaks his thought and the woman acts out her love. Lacan's text comes first, he does not need Felman in order to know what he wants to say, then to say it and later to have it published; but, if one is to take seriously what he says, he does need her and others like her so that he can experience himself as a subject, can have somewhere for his question to go.

Language is performative, it produces an effect. This might be the effect of understanding, or it might – therapeutically, for example – move us on into a different dimension of activity. In his speech and its record in writing, Lacan performs continually, addresses language so intimately that there often seems to be nothing there but performance, an evocation of something constantly slipping away. Some of the effects of this will be explored more fully in Chapter 4, but one thing Lacan's enigmatic performance does evoke, quite deliberately, is the idea of the unconscious. For this attribute of being in perpetual motion, never solid enough to be fully grasped, is taken by psychoanalysts of various schools of thought to be characteristic of the unconscious, above and beyond any of its other attributes. The Freudian unconscious is not a place, a kind of storeroom for truth; rather, the unconscious is *dynamic*, it is something that is always active, a source of motivations that make things happen. Unconscious ideas are mobile and disruptive, constantly pushing for expression, only forced into silence by the equally vivacious and oftentimes desperate activities of the mechanisms of defence. Give these ideas an inch and they will take a mile, and then no-one can know what demons will be invoked, in what way consciousness and ordinary behaviour will be undermined. Lacan's speech attempts to reproduce this state in an explicit and paradoxically conscious way, as it articulates the message that the unconscious is always operating, even when discourse appears at its most formal and well-organised; and that the effects of the unconscious can be seen in slips and inconsistencies, as everyone knows, but also in linguistic tension and desire.

THE DISCOURSE OF THE OTHER

The potential subversiveness of unconscious mental life is a theme of some significance for thinking about sexual difference. In particular, the unpredictable nature of the unconscious is crucial to the view that it may be creative, bringing something new into existence rather than (as in its effects in psychopathological states, particularly where trauma is at their source) imposing deathly repetition and constraint. In this sense, and contrary to images of the unconscious as the repository of fixed representations of past experience, it should be thought of in the *future tense*, as something unknowable until it occurs, something existent only as a potential, not as a fact. This idea of the unconscious as a potential can be compared with the following statement by Levinas on the nature of the future – indeed, the word 'unconscious' could be substituted in it for the word 'future', to good effect:

The future is not buried in the bowels of a pre-existent eternity, where we would come to lay hold of it. It is absolutely other and new. And it is thus that one can come to understand the very reality of time, the absolute impossibility of finding in the present the equivalent of the future, the lack of any hold upon the future.

(Levinas, 1947, p. 46)

One of the most compelling fantasies about the future is that we can discover it, we can know what is going to happen, because in some way all events about to occur have already occurred, are already known. We only have to find the key, the time machine, then we will be there, in the concreteness of actual events. What Levinas points out, however, is that the future is not in actuality like this: we cannot lay hold of it as if it is lying in wait somewhere, to be discovered, because it is simply not there. It has not yet been made. So, too, with unconscious phenomena: they are not bricks or encapsulated ideas hidden away but in principle discoverable; rather, they are actions – wishes, desires, impulses, things that have effects – called into play as life unfolds. Something happens; that is how we know that the unconscious has been at work.

In the same paper in which Levinas describes the impossibility of grasping the future, he makes the following statement about the relationship with the other:

The relationship with the other is not an idyllic or harmonious relationship of communion, or a sympathy through which we put ourselves in the other's place; we recognise the other as resembling us, but exterior to us; the relationship with the other is a relationship with a Mystery.

(Levinas, 1947, p. 43)

Taking this sentence out of context, I want to think about it in relation to gender. 'We recognise the other (sex) as resembling us, but exterior to us.' We can only look in at the other from the outside, knowing that there is something there that is a link, but that a chasm exists between us – a wilderness which might in principle be crossed, but in practice defeats most travellers. Levinas' original statement applies to all relationships, but there is something additional that the introduction of sexual difference brings to it. The question or fantasy is that the wilderness can be crossed to achieve a state of completeness; as will be discussed in later chapters, the fantasy that the other (sex) completes the one (self) arises in response to experiences of desire and lack but is itself a major contributor to the intensity of gender friction. In that sense, the exteriority of the other, as Levinas puts it, 'leads the subject back to itself through light' (*ibid.*): it is necessary for the other (sex) to be different from the one (self), or it would add nothing, no complementarity could be fantasised, still less achieved. Yet, alongside this fantasy of complementarity, we also believe we can know the other, we can face the other sex as an opposite but as one who knows what that opposition means – and the recalcitrance with which each sex refuses to fit into the other's scheme can produce violence as well as desire.

Here are two women's statements about Freud, bearing on the kind of knowledge of sexual difference which is offered by psychoanalysis. The first is again from Felman.

> Freud's discovery of the unconscious is the outcome of his being capable of reading in the hysterical discourse of the other his own unconscious. The discovery of the unconscious was Freud's discovery, within the discourse of the other, of what was actively reading within himself.
>
> (Felman, 1987, p. 60)

The second quotation is from Toril Moi.

> Psychoanalysis is born in the encounter between the hysterical woman and the positivist man of science. It is in this reversal of the traditional roles of subject and object, of speaker and listener, that Freud more or less unwittingly opens the way for a new understanding of human knowledge. But the psychoanalytical situation is shot through with paradoxes and difficulty. For if Freud's (and Breuer's) act of listening represents an effort to *include* the irrational discourse of femininity in the realm of science, it also embodies their hope of *extending* their own rational understanding of psychic phenomena. *Grasping* the logic of the unconscious they want to make it accessible to reason.
>
> (Moi, 1989, pp. 196–7)

Felman's emphasis is on the reflexiveness of Freud's project, the way in which its trajectory was one in which self-discovery and investigation of others were interwoven. This largely occurred across the sexual divide: as will be explored in Chapter 3, the neurotic phenomena of Freud's mind at times found expression in identification with the female hysterics who were the most productive vein he mined, the original 'subjects' of psychoanalysis. Moreover, Felman seems to be arguing that the gaze Freud turned on these female hysterics was productive precisely because it revealed what was 'reading within himself' – his own unconscious as an act, as a force to make things happen. The discovery of the unconscious in others thus becomes another version of the profound process of self-discovery that so characterised psychoanalysis' beginnings; put another way, the discourse of the hysteric – the feminine discourse of a series of neurotic women – was colonised by Freud as a way of discovering and transforming himself. Across the divide of sex, a gaze penetrates the apparent other and takes back something which is already known, if somewhat obscure. The hysterical female other is used to transform the male self, to produce a knowledge which can then be published abroad.

Moi's conception of the insight of psychoanalysis spells this out, whilst also articulating the ambiguity of the power relationship that pertains. In so doing, she communicates the ambiguity of the psychoanalytic approach to sexual difference itself. In her account, Freud allows the woman hysteric to speak, creating a space in 'science' for the voice of the irrational. This reverses the conventional male/female division – the one in which Lacan says his word and Felman hears it. The hysteric speaks, Freud listens, reflects her speech back to her, makes it visible and meaningful. What she says is not mad any more, it makes sense, it is worthy of respect. At its most subversive, this approach deconstructs the ready-made polarities of traditional western thought; now it is no longer clear that truth equals rationality, that meaning equals sense. But the other side of this is that Freud acts as the one who tames this irrational speech, making it rational, explaining it and taking it over. He quotes the woman, only to know better. This, too, is present in psychoanalysis: interpreting everything, it can make it all as dry as dust, reduce its poetry to the logical formulations of an unconscious 'explained'. Moi says about this ambiguity:

> When the colonising impulse gains the upper hand, psychoanalysis runs the risk of obliterating the language of the irrational and the unconscious, repressing the threatening presence of the feminine in the process . . . But there is also in [Freud's] texts a will to let the madwoman speak, to consider *her* discourse as one ruled by its own logic, to accept the logic of another scene.
>
> (Moi, 1989, p. 197)

Here, then, there is an identification between the discourse of femininity and that of the unconscious; in Felman's account, however, it appears that the unconscious is that of Freud, that his own hysteria is made visible through the woman. But perhaps these two points are not so far apart; for men, the terrifying aspect of irrationality is equivalent to the terrors to be found both in femininity and in the unconscious – both seem exterior, both are potentially outside of control. For women, excluded systematically from power and rationality, made victims of the body, the unconscious is both outside and in, part of the identity foisted upon the self.

Or so it seems: this is the convention of psychoanalysis, that male is same, female other. Indeed, it has traditionally been argued that masculinity is sought and femininity denied. 'The repudiation of femininity', writes Freud (1937, p. 357), 'must surely be a biological fact, part of the great riddle of sex.' In the great formative moment of development, when what is desired and what is allowed collide in the Oedipus complex, the boy's fear is that of castration, of becoming like a woman, of losing the marker of difference. Vacancy beckons, or so it seems. For girls, too, claims Freud, the wish is to be done with the feminine, to be active and empowered like the male. For a while, in the phallic phase of development, they can enjoy the clitoris, thinking it is good enough, then wham! they spot what they want and will spend the rest of their lives chasing after it.

> They notice the penis of a brother or playmate, strikingly visible and of large proportions, and at once recognise it as the superior counterpart of their own small and inconspicuous organ, and from that time forward fall a victim to envy for the penis.
>
> (Freud, 1925a, p. 335)

Even I, a man, wonder about the accuracy of this, so it is no surprise to find a feminine chorus aggressively repudiating the supposed repudiation. First, however, it is worth noting that there is a strong cohort of feminists who do not reject the Freudian account, but who take it on and make it their own. Here, for example, is an extract from an essay by Parveen Adams, writing 'between' feminism and psychoanalysis, but staying with the Freudian orthodoxy at least to some degree:

> Both the boy and the girl have to submit to castration to allow the emergence of desire, that investment of the object with erotic value which makes the object relation possible ... The whole economy of desire is rooted in the phallus *and* this phallus is attributed to the father ... so if desire is the investing of the object with erotic value, this investment is not made in relation to difference as such, but in relation to a gendered difference. The object's erotic value is dependent on the question of whether the man or the woman has the phallus. Desire is *engendered* by difference.
>
> (Adams, 1989, p. 248)

Adams describes the Oedipal theme with logic: given this, then that. The particular logic employed is phallic logic: boy and girl 'submit to castration', creating a gap which is experienced as desire; it is also a process defined by the relationship with the phallus-attributed-to-the-father; this relationship is different for females and males; therefore, desire exists in relation to a gendered difference. This account encapsulates the Freudian idea that at the heart of the individual's psychology lies desire, and this desire is inextricably linked with sexual difference.

But why should a woman want to adopt this argument? There have been some strong, womanly voices in favour of the Freudian/Lacanian assertion that desire is formed out of lack (e.g. Mitchell and Rose, 1982), an assertion that seems to lead ineluctably to a deterministically gendered position on what Adams calls the 'economy of desire'. The significance of this position can only be understood in relation to the oppositional one, in which not just penis envy but the whole argument of the *necessity* of sexual difference is put into question. For instance, here is one of the most articulate modern versions of this viewpoint, written by Hélène Cixous, whose bounteous contempt is levelled at all those approaches that identify desire with lack, that assume, for example, that because the woman is apparently 'lacking' *psychologically*, she wants just the *anatomical* bit she has not got:

> I don't want a penis to decorate my body with. But I do desire the other for the other, whole and entire, male or female; because living means wanting everything that is, everything that lives, and wanting it alive. Castration? Let others toy with it. What's a desire originating from a lack? A pretty meagre desire.
>
> (Cixous, 1976, p. 262)

She wants everything, this hungry woman, and she wants it without sexual difference, she wants it 'whole and entire, male or female'. To say it more strongly: she wants to deny the difference.

It is worth considering what this denial of difference might mean, given the emphasis on the irrevocability of sexual division to be found in most psychoanalytic theories – even when a space is allowed for something called 'bisexuality', usually indicating the presence of active and passive modes of sexual gratification, or a possible heterogeneity of sexual objects. Freud (1937) writes that sexual difference is the final point beyond which analysis cannot go, the 'bedrock', the place to which psychoanalysis returns and at which it discovers its therapeutic limit. Although he also discusses the bisexuality of children and the way it is extended into adulthood, he places the Oedipus complex, with its inauguration of the chain of sexual difference, at the centre of the developmental spiral. In Freud's account, the Oedipus complex occurs at what is, in psychoanalytic terms, a relatively late point in development, but its effect is to make the pre-Oedipal bisexuality of the child no longer attainable: it fixes the individual subject in a gendered position from which no escape is allowed. Once one experiences oneself as feminine or masculine, it is no longer possible to imagine oneself in a non-sexed state; imagination itself – even what might seem to be a 'memory' – appears from a position along the divide of sex.

There is, therefore, nothing outside sexual difference, nothing that is not sexed. In Lacan's terms, denial of sexual difference involves denial of the Symbolic – 'foreclosure' – and this is what produces psychosis (Frosh, 1991). Alternatively and relatedly, the belief that one is not sexed can be interpreted as an hysterical belief, in which the female body is substituted for the penis. But it is not just women who want to deny difference: some very famous male psychoanalysts have tried to do the same, even in defiance of their own theories. For example, ' "When it comes down to it," announced Lacan on one occasion to his seminar audience, "I am a perfect hysteric, that is to say, without symptoms, except from time to time mistakes in gender" ' (Heath, 1987, p. 7). Presumably, this is Lacan engaging in more posing and play-acting, this time concerning the possibility of gender-bending, playing with the boundaries of sexual difference when he also argues that sexual difference is the definitional point from which perceptions and experiences are built up. However, there is also something here which is linked with the idea of not wanting to 'lack' anything, but of wanting somehow to transcend division and experience or at least know it all – a state of mind towards which Lacan does not seem to have been averse.

Thus, when Cixous says she wants it all whole, she is being hysterical or psychotic: according to psychoanalysis, that is what is involved in denying the power of sexual division. Her desire is for everything, the whole full jar, because she cannot bear to accept the reality of boundaries. She is also, however, giving voice to something which is a very widespread wish, shared between the sexes. This is the wish to move away from an emphasis on deprivation and towards a celebration of enjoyment – of a desire which is *for* something positive, instead of just 'originating from a lack'. Whether this is being utopian in a forlorn or in a revolutionary sense is one theme for this book, but at least Cixous can 'imagine an elsewhere', and that must be worth doing.

Cixous, then, is representative of a tendency to deny the significance of sexual difference, to see it as an ideological movement constructed to oppress. Her verve is not just subversive, in the way that some feminist writers have undermined phallocentric logic by a playful series of deliberate misreadings and mischievous 'infidelities' (Gallop, 1982); it is also an assertion of the possibility of full desire, a desire rooted in abundance rather than loss, creativity rather than absence. So, her exultant paean to womanhood is sexed, certainly, but also all-encompassing, allowing no lack at all.

> Heterogeneous, yes. For her joyous benefits she is erogenous; she is the erotogeneity of the heterogeneous; airborne swimmer, in flight, she does not cling to herself; she is dispersible, prodigious, stunning, desirous and capable of others, of the other woman that she will be, of the other woman she isn't, of him, of you.
>
> (Cixous, 1976, p. 260)

This exciting abundance is immensely appealing and seductive: we might all want it, want 'her, him and you'. But it is dangerous too, slipping back into a position that promotes the romance of womanhood, its mystique – something that, in the midst of the masculine language that defines desire, subject, object, you, me, masculine and feminine, represents a place of otherness, and of the fulfilment of wishes. This reproduces the picture of the woman as magic and mystery, but also as destructive potential, through which, historically, women have often been idealised and denigrated; it is the woman as poem, as fleeting vision, and as death. No wonder, then, that some women want to remain hard-nosed about it, arguing that these things are illusions, that really there is only sexual difference engendered through lack. They seem to say, 'Don't be taken in by all this; you may subvert it, play with it, but the realities of power are profound, and we need to take them seriously.' Even Cixous recognises this, despite her assertion of feminine ubiquity, as shown by her comment on the real effects of patriarchy: 'Their "Symbolic" exists, it holds power – we, the sowers of disorder, know it only too well' (1976, p. 255).

GETTING BACK TO THE SUBJECT

For a man, there is something strikingly attractive about these debates amongst feminists. This is not just because they split the opposition (so men do not have to change, there are arguments on both sides), but because they have so much verve, such energy – noticeably more than the apologetic posturing of many of the writings of the 'men's movement'. These women write as if hungry with desire; their use of psychoanalysis is embodied, it smells of passion, it is so different from the tortuous conservatism of the clinical institutes of psychoanalysis. If there is still any vestige of radicalism in psychoanalytic thought, it is to be found in these women, and especially when they are French.

The women create a spectacle, they live psychoanalytic radicalism. They use provocative words, they seduce, they express and practise infidelity. They laugh and make others laugh. So much beauty on stage. And they can be generous, too, finding a place for men, asserting that it is not just 'woman' they are talking about, but a femininity that transcends or transgresses sexual division, a femininity which can be lived by both women and men. 'Cixous is quite clear that this concept of "the feminine" is not to be equated with "woman" or with women ... The "feminine" is that which has been repressed, which returns as disruption through the mechanisms of the unconscious' (Shiach, 1989, p. 157). Femininity is defined not as a gender identity, but as a disruptive mode of activity, like the unconscious; it is that disruptiveness which is part of all of us, women and men. Nevertheless, presumably because of their own historical 'repression', it is women who express it best.

This can be understood, however, as another turn of the screw of oppression, in which women are romanced and then marginalised. In most debates on sexual difference, including psychoanalytic debates, it is the women who embody sexuality while the men adhere to reason. When reason alone is insufficient, as it is in emotive encounters and when the relationship stakes are high, men can be left with little to fall back on. In a sense this can be seen as a further castration – with no life in our reason, we are so far removed from our emotions that we cannot breathe any form of desire, whether of lack or of fullness. We have to listen, gratefully, to the passion of the women – gratefully because we can vicariously pick up some life from them, and also because they embody all points of view, so there is some space left for us. But, of course, something quite obvious and conventional is going on here, as it always goes on. While the women indulge in emotion, create excitement and passion and light, the men get on, in our dried-up way, with ruling the world.

The potential double-bind constructed between psychoanalysis and gender is difficult to manage well. If I admire a woman's writing it is in part because she fills the position of the Other to the man – she allows me to breathe through her link with life. The stale order/odour of the phallus is displaced by the verve of the feminine; I can look in on this and enjoy it, without necessarily giving up my own position. But it does also go further than this, producing a way of knowing which contrasts with those usually employed in science and also dominant within psychoanalysis. For instance, the ebullience of some of the writing of psychoanalytic feminists presents a challenge to academic, rational modes of thought and to that approach to psychological phenomena that holds involvement at a distance, looking in on the subject from a position of mastery or knowledge. The whole concept of 'writing the body', in which writers strive to include the rhythms of the (female) body in their texts, is a way of making contact, of linking thought and feeling, which is different both from stereotypically masculine modes of understanding and from some major strands in psychoanalysis. It is an explicit attempt to make texts expressive as well as indicative in order to communicate the 'feel' as well as the appearance of things.

One relatively straightforward way of thinking about this issue is in terms of the gendered components of the domination of *vision* in much psychoanalytic thinking, and the alternatives which might be available. Both Freud and Lacan privilege the visible as the order of knowledge and the motor of development: it is, for example, the *sight* of the boy's penis or the girl's lack that inaugurates the castration complex and the whole arena of sexual difference. Prior to that, in Lacan's developmental scheme, it is when the infant catches sight of her or himself in the mirror that the whole activity and structure of the ego are cranked into operation. Looking, mirrors, images – these, along with language, are the central pillars of Lacanian thought. But there is a way in which sight, and possibly language too, is a distancing mechanism: the act of looking objectifies the other, places it outside the self and holds power over it through negation of its inner life. If one gets too close to something it is hard to see it clearly, to distinguish between what is the object and what the self. Take a step back and the object can be seen in perspective; it can be placed where it belongs in the scheme of things. It is less messy, more in proportion. From the perspective of the one who is observed, the experience of being looked at involves being objectified; this can be turned to advantage in exhibitionism and forms of carnival display, or when one is admired, or indeed through the aggressive assaults on vision characteristic of resistance movements such as punk. But it is never possible fully to control the looker; that is where power lies.

In contrast, the senses of smell, touch and taste seem to be more autonomous, less controllable, and more likely to overwhelm the subject. Subject and object blur much more here: sexual pleasure, for example, particularly in its subversive form as that which Lacanians and others term 'jouissance', is not limitable to the visual register, but involves a losing of self–other boundaries through physical encounter. Repression of odour and taste, of touch and physicality – repression of the sensual component of the sexual – is a characteristic of phallic culture, lost in its admiration for the appearance of power, the 'turgidity' of the phallic object. Because it looks big it must be important; show it around the place and everyone falls on their face and worships. Get close enough to feel, however, and one is lost in the actuality of the other – in their existence as a desiring being. The gendered nature of all this is obvious, but here is a more pronounced version of it:

> Lacan's ocularcentrism – his vision-centredness – in complicity with Freud's, privileges the male body as a phallic, virile body and regards the female body as castrated ... the female can be construed as castrated, lacking a sexual organ, only on the information provided by vision. The other sensori-perceptual organs would have confirmed the presence of a female organ instead of the absence of a male organ.
>
> (Grosz, 1990, p. 39)

A version of the Oedipus complex derived from touch or smell rather than sight might have turned out quite differently.

It is perhaps no accident that the principal psychoanalytic theorist of the physical was a woman, Melanie Klein. Her theory is full of the body, particularly the mother's body: the child is enveloped in it, experiences it as the entire world, structures her or his own consciousness according to direct and phantasised experiences with it. The breast is more powerful than the penis; the infant's phantasy supposedly has the penis contained in (swallowed up by) the breast; and it is the breast as feeding object, as something with which there is a relationship unmediated by sight or language, which is the crucial performative force in the child's early experience. Moreover, throughout development it is the relationship with the breast that is constantly returned to, the breast being a symbol both of power (it is envy directed towards this, not penis envy, that is central to Kleinian thinking on destructiveness), and also of the extent to which the external world can be trusted to help the individual contain her or his own passion.

The key dynamic concepts to be found in Kleinian thought are those of projection and introjection (along with projective and introjective identification), and envy (Segal, 1973; Hinshelwood, 1989; Frosh, 1987a). These are concepts based on metaphors of incorporation and expulsion which in turn are held to be founded on the actual experiences of the infant – the infantile world being dominated by immediate bodily sensations. The inner world is built up on the model not of the outer world, but of sensations of feeding and excreting, and relatedly of being engulfed or abandoned. The outer world is then invested with these qualities through projection, commonly involving projection of pieces of the self into the other. So, distinctively, Kleinians produce a vision of the subject in continuous phantasised contact with the object, so much in contact that boundaries blur and it is possible to feel inside the self what is going on inside the other. The mother and infant are so mutually entangled that the experience of one is incorporated into the experience of the other; this is the prototype for all intense experiences throughout life.

The consequences of this view can be seen clearly in the Kleinian account of transference and countertransference (see Frosh, 1987a). This assumes the possibility of knowledge of the other being available in a form unmediated by language, as a kind of automatic mixing of the unconscious of the analysand into that of the analyst. For Kleinians, the analytic encounter is one in which the patient inserts her or his unconscious states – including entire sections of self as well as specific impulses – 'into' the analyst, whose task it is to hold them, survive their passion and pass them back in an ameliorated form, often linguistically through interpretations, but also (especially when the patient is very disturbed) though the non-verbal elements of the setting. The crucial point here is the interweaving of transference and countertransference: the latter is the reflection of the former, it is the analyst's response to the patient's transference, that is, to what has been placed in her or him by the patient's projective activity.

Thus, just by being there in the room, a finely attuned instrument calibrated to lock onto the patient's projections, the analyst 'knows' the patient's unconscious mind. The capacity to do this comes from infancy, from the experience of being 'held' and understood by the mother, a literal and metaphorical container for the infant's passions. In the work of the post-Kleinian analyst Bion, this notion is well expressed by the idea of 'reverie' (Bion, 1962; Frosh, 1991): a state of mind present in the mother, in which she can accept and manage all the projections she experiences as coming from her infant. In the developmental context, Bion writes:

> Reverie is that state of mind which is open to the reception of any 'objects' from the loved object and is therefore capable of the reception of the infant's projective identifications whether they are felt by the infant to be good or bad.
>
> (Bion, 1962, p. 36)

Reverie is a relationship stance characterised by a receptiveness to all experience, to everything that the child can offer. The Kleinian argument is that the mother acts as a receptacle for the infant's destructiveness as well as for her or his loving impulses; she takes these in and, by surviving them and continuing to be emotionally available to her infant, she communicates the possibility of acceptance and integration. The infant, consequently, experiences her or his destructiveness as managed and therefore manageable, thus becoming more able to tolerate it as an aspect of the self. This state of maternal receptivity is also what characterises the ideal mental state to be sought by the therapist or psychoanalyst: basically an openness to, and a willingness if necessary to be changed by, the patient's experience. Taking in the patient's anxiety, 'holding' and making sense of it whilst remaining calm oneself, giving back to the patient some idea of its meaning – this is the process of containment resulting from the state of reverie. From the point of view of the patient, the experience of being 'contained' in this way is of having one's fragmented self, with all its destructive elements, accepted, tolerated and made manageable, alongside an awareness that this beneficial cycle arises from the presence of a reliable and stable other. Articulation of pain and anxiety, and the projection of destructiveness into the therapist, create a tension which can result in greater integration or in a more desperate splitting. When therapy is successful it is because of the therapist's ability to 'hold' these projections, to recognise and respond to them without retaliating or falling apart. Thus it is that the patient experiences containment, the sense that something – some reparation – can be made of what otherwise might be viewed as inner waste.

The ideal state of mind for the analyst, in this account, is one characterised by an ability to free oneself from conscious knowledge in order to be receptive to what is actually coming into the analyst from the patient. The result of this, in theory, is that the analyst does not need to be 'told' anything, although it is obviously the case that the speech of the patient is the prime carrier of her or his emotion. However, the denotative content of the speech is only a small element in what goes on therapeutically: speech is again performative, in a different sense to that used before, in that it makes the analyst feel something and it is the knowledge of that feeling that is crucial. Once again, this kind of knowledge 'is not constative (cognitive)' (Felman, 1987, p. 119); it is the kind of knowledge which might not always be open to clear articulation, but which can be acted upon and is recognised through its effects.

The genderedness of this needs some further consideration. According to Kleinians, the core capacity for the most profound analytic knowledge and experience of the other is derived from the immersion of the infant in the mother's physicality. It is not looking or even listening that announces the structure of the unconscious and of personal relatedness; it is feeding, incorporation, being held and touched. Indeed, the most primitive and the most advanced states – envy and reverie – are both constructed out of this matrix of physical intertwining, of one along with and in the other. There are phallic elements in this theory, for sure, but it is primarily a theory of experience constructed along the lines of maternity; it is a female theory.

No wonder such passion surrounds it. This passion rests across the dimension mother/father, a dimension of considerable significance in all the discussions in this book. The argument on the side of the mother, represented in the work of Klein, is that the physical, embodied knowledge characteristic of maternity – the child in and coming out from the body, both part of and separate from the self – is the foundational knowledge for true understanding of and linking with the other. Immersion in the other is possible, as revealed in therapy through the activation of projective and introjective identification, processes of giving up parts of the self to the other or incorporating phantasised aspects of the other into the self. The most developed state of understanding is one in which the presence of the other inside the self can be tolerated and reflected upon, translated into language but already known and comprehended before this act of translation takes place. The more traditional Freudian stance of keeping the other at a distance – looking at her or him from a separate point of view – is less useful than emotionally 'holding' and 'containing' the other, to use the favourite terminology of post-Kleinian analysts. This metaphor of physical contact and of the nurturing of infancy makes maternal knowledge central to the attainment of mental health, whether during development or in analysis, and it valorises the ability of the analyst to set aside her or his usual patterns of abstract or distanced thought and return to a set of embodied feelings.

There is much to be said in favour of this view. It makes therapists work to understand themselves and resolve their own conflicts, in recognition of the significance of what might be termed the 'calibration of the unconscious', the ability to reflect on the feelings they have during therapeutic sessions and on what these feelings might mean in terms of the process of the therapy itself. So, for example, the sense of being completely stuck and unable to say anything useful, coupled with an underlying anger and despair, becomes a state of mind to be examined for its relationship to what the patient may be feeling, rather than to be acted out either by blaming the patient for her or his stupidity in not being able to change, or blaming oneself for the poverty of one's therapeutic skills. The countertransference-driven Kleinian approach also makes it very difficult to escape into the conventional defence of intellectualisation, creating a theory about something as a means of taking away its sting.

On the other hand, there are some troubling aspects to the model. For one thing, the imagery of the maternal evoked by Kleinian writing is quite conventional. Kleinians do not romanticise motherhood in quite the way some others do, for instance Winnicott (Frosh, 1987a); they are too keen on the negative, destructive components of the human psyche to do that. They do not assume that mothering is easy, natural, or automatically beautiful. Nevertheless, they do use the assumed connectedness of the mother with her baby as a model of human knowledge – immersion of one in the other, the assumed ability to transcend bodily boundaries and directly experience the unconscious contents of the other's mind. There is a different kind of romance here, to be found in the portrayal of the mother who automatically 'knows' her baby, is absolutely in tune with her or him and loves the baby so profoundly that she can tolerate all her or his feelings, whether they be of love or hate. The mother is portrayed as long-suffering and full of generous responsiveness to all the baby's demands; a responsiveness which does not have to be articulated in language for it to be perceptible and for it to have its effects. This is 'romantic' not just in the sense of being at variance with the actuality of most mothers' experience, but also in the related sense that it is an image connected with wishes rather than truth. What the study of narcissism suggests (Frosh, 1991) is that the wish to be perfectly understood by, and at one with, a caring and containing other is extremely common, perhaps even universal, and relates to the presumed infantile experience of incorporation in the other. The idea that mothering actually consists in such a perfect understanding is taken up quite crudely in some object relations theories; as mentioned above, Kleinians are not so crude, but they nevertheless invoke the narcissistic fantasy and present it as a picture of the ideal.

There is something else about this which should be considered, relating to power. The assumption that it is possible to understand another fully, to attune oneself to her or his unconscious wishes by means of projective and introjective activity, without this being properly articulated and thought about, is an assumption that can lead to a state of 'knowingness' in the oppressive sense – being 'knowing' about the other, on the basis of no public evidence. You come into the consulting room and I feel something; this allows me to 'know' you. The apparent certainty here should be mistrusted, the suggestion repelled that one can ever be in possession of the patient's truth through direct, unmediated experience – that the patient's unconscious can mingle with the analyst's in an automatic way, crossing the self–other wilderness and dispensing with physical and psychological boundedness. It is one thing to strive hard to comprehend the other's unspoken feeling, but if the difficulty and unreliability of this process are not articulated, if instead there is proposed a magical link between self and other which is not open to scrutiny because it is a matter of boundary dissolution and feeling, only commented upon retrospectively, then the possibilities for abuse of power are greatly heightened. Kleinians do often seem very certain of their knowledge, not sustaining a receptive state of 'not-knowing' at all; in being like this, there is always the danger that they will silence the other when she or he is struggling most uncertainly to speak.

Considering the apparently magical connection between infant and mother in terms of an imaginary relationship, a fantasy about what kind of connectedness is possible, leads into another strand in the gender debate. This starts with the particular rendering of the psychoanalytic concept of narcissism mentioned in outline above. Grunberger's (1989) account is useful here. He traces the origins of the regressive longings characteristic of the narcissistic state of mind to the early experience of the infant with what he terms the 'monad', a post-natal recreation of the pre-natal state of absorption in the mother, the function of which is to protect the infant against too rapid exposure to the pressure of her or his internal drives and the unmediated impact of the outer world.

> The monad is a nonmaterial womb which functions as though it were material; on the one hand it encloses the child in its narcissistic universe; on the other, it prepares it for the partial dissolution of that universe – or, in other words, for the dissolution of its own essence.
>
> (Grunberger, 1989, p. 3)

The intense experience of life 'in' the monad is something which remains with the human throughout life, coded into the deepest recesses of subjectivity and producing a pull back towards its totally protected state. It is this which is taken by Grunberger to be at the source of all attempts to become 'at one' with the other, to enter into an ideal state of pure bliss – and, as such, to become part of a world of fantasy in which conflict and contradiction are denied.

> Given that it is part of his subjective reality, man will go on demanding to return to the ideal state he experienced in the womb and in a sense, he continued to experience in the monad.
>
> (Grunberger, 1989, p. 12)

The wish for perfect harmony with the other is thus a wish for a return, a regressive wish. Elsewhere, I have examined the relationship between this version of narcissism and the idea of a 'culture of narcissism' that has infiltrated some of the discussions on contemporary social experience (Frosh, 1991). Here, what should be stressed is the genderedness of Grunberger's account and the way it undercuts the very different Kleinian version of development. Whilst recognising its functional value in early life, Grunberger makes the monad the culprit for regressive narcissism, which in turn is opposed for its renunciation of reality and its impulse towards wishing away all opposition. This wishing away, he claims, can at times take a murderous form, as in the pursuit of purity (racial and otherwise) at all costs that is characteristic of fascist ideology. In this reading, regressive narcissism has at its source the monad, which is

Grunberger's rendering of the maternal dimension that is in some respects extolled in the Kleinian imagery outlined earlier – the imagery of incorporation and total comprehension, of holding and containing and accepting, of pre-verbal links. By contrast, Grunberger presents the Oedipus complex as the route to acceptance of reality: it is through the Oedipal encounter that toleration of otherness is achieved, the prospect of conflict is acknowledged, and reality can therefore be confronted and worked through. As can be seen in the following quotation, this is a vision of development which is also a moral vision, in which the Oedipus complex and its association with the paternal dimension are preferred to the narcissism associated with the mother:

> The Oedipal person reacts to failure as a stimulus to attempt the fulfilment of his Oedipal wishes with renewed determination, but for the narcissist there is no next time, since he prefers the disappearance of the system in which the injury took place . . . He will not try to triumph over the father (to identify with him in order to surpass him later) but will try to abolish the principle of paternity itself and the whole frame of reference of which it was the organiser.
>
> (Grunberger, 1989, p. 39)

The progression described here is from mother to monad to intolerance of conflict, to denial of the father, to the abolition of otherness – to the disavowal of reality.

There is a deep tension in all this, which cannot easily be resolved. The Kleinian image of maternity is not straightforward: the early mother–infant relationship is replete with contradictions and conflicts, with the pain of envy and the destructive capacities inherent in both members of that dyad. The mother's job certainly does not seem easy; and her task of managing the child's projections and remaining whole, as a self and as an object available to the child, looks to be a Herculean one. Yet, within the therapeutic field, the imagery of holding and containing, of reverie, and of an unmediated understanding of the other available through counter-transference, refers back to a different conceptualisation of the mother, in which her physicality and bodily unity with the infant lay the foundations for a perfect understanding of the infant over and above what is available through language. Grunberger's strictures then apply: that this imagery of oneness is part of the regressive urge to deny the necessity of difference, the impossibility of reaching the other with confidence.

But Grunberger's maternal–paternal opposition is less complex than at times it seems. Its misogyny arises not so much from the association between monad and mother, but from its explicit view that the maternal dimension is inferior to the paternal, and that the former is involved in the denial of 'reality' which occurs if the Oedipal conflict is denied, thence leading to narcissism and totalitarianism. The confident relegation of maternity to the arena of fantasy and concomitant promotion of paternity to that of reality are rather distinctively ideological, even if they carry with them an important analysis of the dangers of romantic valorisation of states of purity and utopian wholeness. What Grunberger seems to suggest is that reality, dirty and full of conflict as it is, is a triangulated state in which the paternal principle operates to break up infantile fantasies of rest and rescue; and also that avoidance of this reality is the same as a return to the mother, with potentially catastrophic consequences. The question arises, why should the imagery of the mother be fantasy, and regressive fantasy at that, whilst that of the father is for real? Another psychoanalyst keen on the father, Lacan, has something to say on this.

THE LACANIAN PRINCIPLE

Lacan's opposition to the idealisation of maternity and the mothering imagery present in object relations theory and its Kleinian relatives, is incorporated into his account of the Imaginary and Symbolic orders of human subjectivity. These 'orders' have proved to be strikingly resonant for thinking about the practice of analysis and also about the phenomena of contemporary culture, partly because of their concern with modes of representation (particularly vision and language), but also because their content is unexpected, utilising some traditional components of Freudian psychoanalysis (narcissism and the Oedipus complex) for ends that undermine many assumptions about psychological process and structure – and about the aims and principles of psychoanalysis itself.

Describing and explaining the concepts of Imaginary and Symbolic is a task taken on by many authors and does not require repetition here (see Benvenuto and Kennedy, 1986; Grosz, 1990; Frosh, 1987a, 1989). At its simplest, the Imaginary can be thought of as an indicator of a way of experiencing in which the connectedness of things is asserted, in which the possibilities of integration of the self and full linkage with the other are imagined to be attainable. Developmentally, Lacan links this with the mirror phase, in which the child's observation of its representation by the other is taken as the definitional point of its own subjectivity – prior to sexual division, prior to language. There are various senses in which this is 'imaginary': it is concerned with images ('the imago'), it designates a feat of active mental transformation of observed phenomena (a feat 'of imagination'), and it is about a non-real, impossible connection with the other (an 'imaginary' occurrence). This last sense is the most significant here: the unmediated link with the other, the idea that one subject can be wholly recognised in the gaze of the other and fully known to her or him, is something imaginary, something which cannot be maintained in the face of the actual structures of language and material experience.

Felman (1987) makes a helpful point here concerned with the apparent opposition between binary and triangular thought, between narcissism and the Oedipus complex. The first part of this is directly related to the discussion of projection and introjection outlined above in the context of Kleinian thinking on the therapeutic process. The Kleinian description seems to suggest a symmetrical relationship between projection and introjection – the one being the placing of inner psychic material into an external object, the other being the incorporation of the object's mental processes into the self. Kleinian therapy binds the one with the other in an interactive, mutually interpenetrating process, a parallel of the infantile situation in which introjection follows projection constantly, at the same level of complexity. Felman quotes from Lacan's Seminar I (1953–4) on this as follows:

> In the way we use it in analysis, introjection is not the opposite of projection. It is practically employed . . . only when what is at stake is symbolic introjection. It is always accompanied by a symbolic denomination. Introjection is always the introjection of the discourse of the Other, and this fact produces a dimension altogether different from the dimension of projection.
>
> (Felman, 1987, p. 111)

Let us take this quotation alongside a second one, this time from Felman herself.

> The psychoanalytic narrative is nothing other, for Lacan, than the story of, precisely, the discovery of the third participant in the structure of the dialogue. And this dramatic, narrative and structural discovery implicitly refers to Oedipus.
>
> (Felman, 1987, p. 127)

'Nothing other' and 'precisely': Felman is concerned to maximise the force of Lacan's commitment to the triangulation of experience present in his concept of the Symbolic. One can only presume that this is because it is nothing other than the core of the theory, at least in Felman's view, and that it addresses precisely the difference between the Lacanian perspective and that of other psychoanalysts. It is a major contribution, in other words, to the theory of analytic practice.

Lacan asserts that projection should be differentiated from introjection, that the former operates in the register of the Imaginary while the latter operates in the Symbolic. Projection is expulsion of material in such a way that the subject fantasises that it enters directly into the other; as such, it is akin to the Kleinian idea of the unmediated I–thou experience of absorption in the mother or the analyst. Introjection, by contrast, at least 'In the way we use it in analysis', is of something symbolised and other: it is the subject's incorporation of her or his own message after it has been worked on by the analyst, that is, once it has become embedded in the 'discourse of the Other'. What is crucial about this is that it is a way of giving language to the analysand by destabilising fantasies of the Imaginary to reveal the workings of the Symbolic. It introduces the analysand to the impossibility of any complete fulfilment of desire, revealing this to be part of the condition of being a socially structured subject. Forrester's description of the relationship between the Other and what Lacanians term 'full speech' is relevant here. The 'big Other', he writes:

> is the locus of the linguistic code, the guarantee of meaning, the third party in any dual relationship – whether it be analysis or love. The subject's speech is vouched for by his Other . . . Yet it is transformed in having to pass via the fantasy structure in which the ego and its (fantasy-) relations to its objects predominate. The relation of the subject to the Other is thus the main line of the unconscious, for which analysis aims to clear the way.
>
> (Forrester, 1987, p. 71)

Analysis aims to help the subject find the 'main line of the unconscious', which resides not in the I–thou relationship but in the recognition of the third party, that which stands outside the immediate link with the other and acts as 'guarantee' of its meaning. Structurally speaking, this is the father in the Oedipus complex, the Law that articulates and enforces which relationships are allowed and which are not – what can be fulfilled and what only desired. Speaking with the analyst in such a way as to deny or by-pass this triangulation is to engage in empty speech, the speech of one alienated ego to another who cannot answer. Operating with the discourse of the Other, in contrast, is to ask one's question in such a way as to experience the necessity of symbolisation and the struggle for some kind of recognition in language.

This brings us back to the question of expressiveness in psychoanalytic language with which this chapter began – and to Lacan's statement that, 'What I seek in speech is the response of the other'. Except now this otherness has been displaced from the immediate other to that which stands outside and gives meaning to the system of relationships itself. In the Lacanian scheme, this is read in Oedipal terms and is therefore gendered as the Law of the Father, symbolised by the actions of what Lacan terms the 'primary signifier', the phallus.

What is central to the Lacanian argument is the dismissal of the imagery of immediate knowledge of the other as an Imaginary phenomenon, and its replacement with the assertion that human subjecthood is conferred by the activity of the phallus as signifier, acting as an element in the Oedipus-castration drama. As noted above, this is explicitly gendered; it also acts as the inaugurator of sexual difference that then reaches back through childhood to create a situation in which a non-gendered position is irrecoverable. Thus, the 'accession to the Symbolic', as it is often termed, is also the accession to a sexed position in language and culture, a sexed subjectivity. Following this through, it appears that the activity of the paternal signifier, the phallus, subverts the maternal Imaginary; the possibility of a non-linguistic, bodily based comprehension of the other is dismissed as an idealisation. As with Grunberger's argument, the maternal is therefore viewed as regressive, even if it is also functional developmentally; the paternal is where true subject-status resides.

There are numerous complexities involved in the Lacanian discourse on sexual difference, many of them located in the concept of the 'phallus', which will be the central topic for Chapter 4. The comparison with Grunberger's work brings one of these to the fore, however, and this is particularly germane to the contrast with Kleinian thought. Grunberger seems to suggest that there is a relatively unproblematic entity, 'reality', which is characterised by conflict and contradiction but which is tangible, indeed less imaginary than the narcissistic condition. For Lacan, such a reality is not so easy to define. His concept of 'the Real' refers to a non-recoverable early state of biologically given fusion which itself is never observable, as the subject is always structured by the desire of others even from before birth. The phallus is also not an entity but a 'signifier', something performative rather than absolute. Nevertheless, Lacanians continue to assert that language and culture are structured according to the operations of the paternal Law, a position that suggests some absoluteness about what actually happens, what is the 'real' structure of the Symbolic. This is a position, too, that excludes femininity, or at least marginalises it, so that at times the category 'woman' becomes elided with the category of the 'Other'. All this material is very confusing and requires some sorting out; much of this book is an attempt to deal with it. At its simplest, however, it suggests that the apparent certainty of the Kleinian account of countertransference – that one can know the other from the inside – is undermined by the tricky activity of symbolisation: one can only begin to know the other through the mediation of the other, and this produces uncertainties, misrecognitions, and wildernesses which cannot be crossed. And in this process, sexual division, despite its own ambiguity, is one of the strongest structural markers.

Chapter 3

Inside the dream

THE ORIGINS OF PSYCHOANALYSIS

In Chapter 2, I argued that sexual difference can only be fully explored through tracing its effects, through giving body to it and making it material. Whatever one says about sexual difference, the way of saying it becomes an expression of how that difference is being experienced; as one speaks so one is positioned, male or female, with all the accompanying associations of mastery or resistance, knowing or being, sight or touch. This does not mean that sexual difference 'is' anything absolutely fixed; rather, the organisation of the social world around difference produces people in relation to gender, so that what are in principle 'empty' categories (masculine, feminine) become filled with expectations, stereotypes and projections. This does not, however, make their effects any the less real: though gender distinctions may be constructed and in important senses 'arbitrary', they have a hold over us and are difficult, perhaps impossible, to transcend. The tension referred to in Chapter 1 operates here, that as one explores the way in which sexual difference is constructed, seeing this as a social process, so the centrality of gender to subjectivity – to, for example, people's core sense of identity – comes to the fore. Consequently, writing about sexual difference never turns out to be a neutral activity: it always brings one face to face with one's own investments and desires.

Psychoanalysis, too, participates in this process. One of its most forceful teachings is that every discourse has its subtext, its underside or antagonist positioned within it; this subtext speaks through the cracks, through the moments of slippage and uncertainty in language, always calling the whole into question. Just as this is true of the discourse of the analysand, so it is true of the discourse of psychoanalysis itself. At any moment, what is 'really' being said might not be what is apparently being talked about, but something other, something which requires interpretation to bring it out from its hidden place. Moreover, that which does the speaking may not be the composed authorial 'self' which seems to be there, perhaps presenting a face of rationality and equanimity, but it may be – indeed it is likely to be – something unconscious, caught up in complex investments, including those that surround sexual difference. The surface of psychoanalytic language, like that of the language of any analysand, thus masks something significant; and this something is itself momentary and slippery, speaking from a position of uncertainty, of constant change and conflict.

The traditional association of masculinity with rationality and femininity with irrationality begins to apply here. As was described in Chapter 2, there is a sense in which the origins of psychoanalysis can be said to lie in the tension between masculine reason and feminine expressiveness, felt particularly as hysteria: in psychoanalysis, the former speaks of the latter, but it needs the latter if it is to have any specific content. Psychoanalysis is constructed on this knife edge: it plays with the borders of reason, refusing to give up its search for meaning but also showing how unreason is an intrinsic element in the human condition, and will never disappear. Not surprisingly, therefore, even when psychoanalysis is at its most masterful and apparently clearly scientific, it can also be obscure and uncomfortable with itself, suggesting a state of inner unease.

This situation becomes particularly poignant when the implicit parallel between femininity and the unconscious is brought into the open. Translated into gender terms, the apparently 'masculine' activity of knowing and ordering phenomena is always in a relationship with the supposedly 'feminine' activity of embodiment and disruption. When it speaks, in its many contradictory voices, of sexual difference, psychoanalysis delineates concepts that help in the struggle to find meaning and to make sense of the way in which gender insinuates itself into people's psychic lives. But the speech of psychoanalysis also *expresses* this presence of gender. In the texts of psychoanalysis, just as in the discourse of patients, there can be found the voices of sexual difference, channelling, influencing and undermining the narratives which unfold. Indeed, because of its concern with sexuality and subjectivity, the language of psychoanalysis is a particularly sexed language, marked by the slipperiness of its identificatory positions and its playfulness when faced with issues of reference. Whenever it speaks in an apparently 'masculine' voice, it also raises the question of femininity: as the word of the master is put forward, so the subversion of that word appears in the background.

In this chapter, I explore this ambiguity in the gender position of psychoanalysis itself by looking at the way the issue of sexual difference appears in the most important of the foundational texts of psychoanalysis, Freud's *Interpretation of Dreams*.[1] In particular, I argue that this text works with conventional categories of masculinity and femininity in such a way that both sides of the tension referred to above are visible – both how sexual difference acts as an organising principle central to personal identity, and how its constructed character makes transgression of conventional gender categorisation possible. In relation to psychoanalysis, the workings of this text are not simply of historical importance. Throughout its history, psychoanalysis has been caught up with the personality as well as the ideas of Freud. His domination over the movement has been profound both in life and in death. Whilst developments in theory and practice since his time have been very great, Freud's work continues to define the basic principles of analytic theory and practice, and his person continues to be an object of identification, the corporate super-ego of all who have come after him. Moreover, psychoanalysis is an unusual science in that its early body of knowledge was built up in considerable part on the basis of Freud's personality and self-scrutiny. His famous 'self-analysis', carried out in the closing years of the nineteenth century, is commonly represented (particularly by Jones (1955) in the first 'official' biography) as the heroic founding act of psychoanalysis; given that it is explicitly concerned with Freud's subjective impulses and internal struggles, this means that his own conscious and unconscious desires are set up as the marker from which all analysis takes its stance. Freud's self-analysis subsequently became the prototype of the training analysis undergone as part of the process of becoming a psychoanalyst, producing a dynastic sequence begun with the act of self-creation. Already here can be found some structural ambiguities paralleling those encountered in sexual difference. Much as in the Biblical Genesis tale, the original creator contains within his one being all that is necessary for generating life, both male and female elements, one might say; later on, the divisions occur, differentiation begins and no-one can manage the creative analytic task on her or his own.

It is *The Interpretation of Dreams* which is most closely tied to this self-analysis, and which consequently expresses most forcefully the ambiguities and tensions involved in the creative process out of which psychoanalysis was born. In this book, published at the start of the twentieth century, can be found a text which is at once scientific and confessional, incorporating formal theory alongside conscious personal revelation (it is built up mainly around interpretations of Freud's own dreams, as well as those of some of his patients) and unconscious anxiety and desire. And right at the heart of this text, as this chapter will try to show, is an uncertainty over gender: a masculinity that plays with, represses and expresses, its own fragmentation and ambivalent feminine identifications. *The Interpretation of Dreams* is presented by Freud as a triumphant elucidation of the obscure recesses of the irrational – the unknown country of the night; but it raises continually the question of the sexual identity of dreamer and interpreter, and indeed of the dream and its analysis.

All the dreams of his own reported by Freud in the first edition of this great, sprawling book were dreamt during the closing years of the nineteenth century, during a period of struggle for Freud out of which something new was born, something terrible and yet exhilarating – something therefore characteristic of the nature of the modern experience itself. As such, these dreams and their interpretation can be seen as a kind of commentary not only on the situation in which Freud perceived himself to be, but also on the forces and social experiences that gave rise to the great modernist movements of the early twentieth century – forces which are most easily characterised as 'revolutionary', as a breaking out from the constraints of the past into a set of circumstances in which change occurred at an unprecedented pace, often through a radical inversion of belief or social organisation. Images of volcanic upheaval, of the blowing apart of the outworn fabric of centuries by a new, exciting yet dangerous, energy are to be found in many cultural representations (literature, music, art and politics) during this and the immediately following historical period. They are found also in personal psychology and in the manner in which this is expressed in psychoanalytic theory, which stands out as one of the clearest attempts to conceptualise the mental condition of people living through such times (see Frosh, 1991). They are also to be found in Freud's thought.

Anzieu comments thus on Freud's state of mind at the moment of the dreaming (in 1895) of his most famous dream, his 'specimen' dream of Irma's injection (to be discussed more fully below):

> Freud, fragmented into disparate pieces, was searching for his true unity. The system of identifications that had governed him up to then crumbled away. So far, his life had been dominated by the wishes of others. During that night of July 23–24 1895, his dream questioned him about his own wishes.
>
> (Anzieu, 1975, p. 132)

This image of the individual in fragments, no longer assured of the truth of received wisdom and the 'system of identifications' by which he has previously lived, desperately searching for an alternative, unifying meaning that will make it possible to forge a newly integrated life – this is a characteristic modernist image of the individual struggling with the fragmentation of modernity and trying, through his creativity, to win through. It is also presented as a predominantly masculine image of heroic self-construction, in which the individual has sufficient power to force something new into the world, to 'cast off his moorings', as Anzieu terms it (p. 146), and find a new route for himself. Yet even in this there is sexual ambiguity. Freud's task at this time was that of letting go of the traditions of scientific objectivity and social constraint and beginning to study himself, finding a sure voice to articulate his own experience – a task of self-expression and 'identity politics' quite closely associated with contemporary feminism. More specifically, Anzieu terms the consequence for Freud of the questioning process set in motion by the Irma dream an eventual 'second birth' (which 'cannot fail to evoke for him his first birth'

– p. 146), symbolised by the displaced gynaecological examination in the dream itself (looking down Irma's throat to find 'some remarkable curly structures which were evidently modelled on the turbinal bones of the nose' – Freud (p. 182); Freud later notes (p. 194) how Fliess connected 'the turbinal bones and the female organs of sex'). The imagery here is of Freud giving birth to himself anew, releasing an energy that produces psychoanalysis in its wake. The sexuality of this is a combined one, both the single-minded genius and the maternal giving forth; in addition, there is an hermaphrodite sense of the new Freud sliding out from inside the skin of the old.

Freud himself is less delicate and more in tune with the revolutionary feelings of the time. He admits (p. 306) to having wanted to head the chapter on therapy in the book with the caption 'Flavit et dissipati sunt' – 'He blew and they were scattered'. Whether this refers to the problems inherent in his clinical and theoretical work, to his opponents or to the whole established order of things, the imagery here is that of the revolution. The origins of psychoanalysis lie not so much in a birth, it would seem, as in a bomb.

MASCULINE IDENTIFICATIONS: FROM JOSEPH TO MOSES

This terrible beauty that is born. It is with *The Interpretation of Dreams* that psychoanalysis comes into possession of its distinct voice, the voice of the unconscious and the voice of Freud's personality. Freud stamps his authority on his material; he shows how it all fits together, he solves the secret of dreams, he knows what only prophets know. And from this arises a movement of believers, a body of knowers, those who, because of Freud, can see, can interpret and understand.

The religious imagery of this description is one which derives directly from a conscious strategy of identification adopted by Freud himself. This strategy produces an authorial position which is explicitly masculine, unquestioned as such throughout the text, and which also allows Freud to write himself into a connection with his Jewish cultural heritage, so that he becomes a new prophet – secular, maybe, but walking firmly in the footsteps of Old Testament heroes. It seems clear that both these impulses are of great importance to Freud. The question of masculinity is one which, as will be described more fully below, arises for Freud in the context of his attempt to work through his relationship with his father. As such, one trajectory of *The Interpretation of Dreams* might be said to be Freud's attempt to enter into his masculinity – to resolve the issues preventing him from completing the transition from the position of son (to his actual father and the idealised male tutors of his past) to that of father (to his own intellectual legacy, the psychoanalytic movement). In order to do this, Freud adopts identifications which play on the son/father dynamic, particularly in relation to the Biblical figures Joseph and Moses. One of the ironies that emerges here, however, is that the construction of this self-consciously and rather stereotypically 'masculine' persona is constantly in tension with a set of implicit 'feminine' identifications, again expressing the instability of that taken-for-granted polarity.

The second of the impulses mentioned above, that of inserting himself into the cultural heritage of his people, was something that accompanied Freud throughout his life's work. It can be seen in various ways, for example in the impact of his own experiences of anti-semitism (attested to directly in *The Interpretation of Dreams*), the congeniality of his links with other Jewish doctors and laymen (as in his membership of the Bnai Brith organisation), his anxieties over the concentration of Jews amongst the early psychoanalysts, or his response to Nazism. Freud's Jewish background has also been claimed to have had a substantial effect on the content of his theories, particularly in relation to mystical traditions (Bakan, 1958) and, pertinently here, to Jewish ideas on feminine sexuality (Roith, 1987). Whatever the direct influence of these factors, the tone and content of much of *The Interpretation of Dreams* is Biblical, as if Freud is attempting to use the elements of his Jewish background in creating his own book of origins. Moreover, because the pattern of identifications in which this becomes material is a masculine one, the book becomes in part an engagement with patriarchy.

It is worth exploring how the text works here in more detail. Freud's tumultuous arrogance and consciousness of his transitional historical position – between the old and the new, between Egypt and Israel – leads him to identifications with two central Biblical figures, Joseph the seer and Moses the liberator. On the former, Freud writes:

> It will be noted that the name Josef plays a great part in my dreams . . .
> My own ego finds it very easy to hide itself behind people of that name,
> since Joseph was the name of a man famous in the Bible as an interpreter
> of dreams.
>
> (Freud, p. 624, n. 2)

Joseph's gift comes from God and is dependent on his faith in God; exercising it leads him into exile and then to redemption, a process which is later recapitulated (but in reverse) by his entire people. Moses comes at the end of this sequence; Moses comes too at various points in Freud's life, most poignantly at its end, in his muddled and evocative meditation on Nazism, *Moses and Monotheism* (see, for example, Diller, 1991; Bakan, 1958, for extended discussions of the Moses figure in Freud's work and life). In *The Interpretation of Dreams*, Moses appears explicitly for the first time as a figure of identification in one of the 'Rome' dreams:

> Another time someone led me to the top of a hill and showed me Rome

half-shrouded in mist; it was so far away that I was surprised at my view of it being so clear. There was more in the content of the dream than I feel prepared to detail; but the theme of 'the promised land seen from afar' was obvious in it.

(Freud, pp. 282–3)

Moses leads his people out of the slavery of Egypt – the physical oppression, the loss of identity, the false gods – and into the wilderness; but his own arrogance and rebelliousness rule him out from being the one who can take the Israelites into the promised land; he can only glimpse it from afar. Nevertheless, on the way he has given his people the Law; now what they must do to achieve their sovereignty and true status is to follow it. That this proves, in the long term, to be an impossible task is simply one of the conditions of human existence.

There is a great deal of reflexivity in the way Joseph and Moses appear in *The Interpretation of Dreams*; that is, through being significant (highly cathected, in Freudian terminology) figures in a dream landscape, they express a great deal about the text itself, and of course about Freud. Joseph's is a personal vision in which the future troubles of a people become entwined; it is as if they are sucked into the vortex of his own dreams and ambitions. The favoured son (like Freud the first-born of his father's second wife) Joseph dreams immense dreams of grandeur and ambition. Being the chosen of his father, he is abused and enslaved, he arouses envy and desire, he is imprisoned and chained. Then, at the lowest point of his fortune, he discovers his great gift, a magical ability to see into the heart of the mystery of dreams. Through his own awareness of his inner struggle, Joseph learns to be aware of others, and to master them. In interpreting others' dreams so that their structure and meaning is made clear, he realises his own dreams and becomes the master of his brothers. Their envy turns to fear and gratitude, their murmuring is silenced; Joseph's attainments are evidence that his grandeur was no fantasy after all. All this has the structure of a dream itself, a straightforward wish-fulfilment in which the denigrated weakling triumphs over his oppressors. It resonates through *The Interpretation of Dreams* as a response to a memory produced in response to the 'Count Thun' dream. At the age of 'seven or eight', Freud urinates in his parents' bedroom; angered, his father dismisses all previous intimations of greatness with the prophecy: 'The boy will come to nothing.' Freud comments:

This must have been a frightful blow to my ambition, for references to this scene are still constantly recurring in my dreams and are always linked with an enumeration of my achievements and successes, as though I wanted to say: 'You see, I *have* come to something'.

(Freud, p. 309)

The structure of the Joseph story and the recurrent slippage between Freud's conflicts around his own father (discussed further below), and his ambivalence towards his sometime patron and collaborator Josef Breuer, allows Freud to make the same assertion – 'I *have* come to something' – and legitimise his grandiosity and claim to fame.

There is, however, a dark side to Joseph with which Freud seems also to have made a personal connection. Joseph excites envy and recrimination through his complete lack of humility. Living in a dream world, he forces reality to do his bidding, to fulfil the triumphant wishes of his early life. In so doing, he saves his family and his people from famine, only for them to be precipitated into a long nightmare of slavery and despair. The ambiguity of this story – the way personal triumph turns later into communal tragedy – is something deeply engrained in Freud's Jewish consciousness (see Diller, 1991). In relation to *The Interpretation of Dreams* and the founding of psychoanalysis, it is also a poignant expression of doubt: is this all just Freud's dream, and into what nightmare will it lead those who become caught up in it? It is hard, retrospectively, not to see some inner awareness of the forces that later gave rise to Nazism at work here, some unconscious expression of Freud's explicit recognition of, and discomfort with, the link between psychoanalysis and Judaism, and terror of where that might lead. At least, it suggests that Freud's double challenge to the world by first outlining an outrageous theory (dreams are sexual wish-fulfilments) and, secondly, explicitly linking it with his Jewishness, was in part a reaction to his sense of rejection by the scientific and non-Jewish communities.

Moses makes the reverse journey from that of Joseph, from Egypt to the borders of Canaan, from slavery to a freedom bounded by law. He takes with him the bones of Joseph, in order to bury them where they belong, at the end of the long night of exile. The relationship between time and space here is a very complex one, intimately bound up with the relationship of dream to reality. On leaving Egypt, Moses takes his people into the wilderness; failing to have perfect faith, the generation of people who were slaves are required to die out before a new generation, knowing nothing of their former status in Egypt, can be relied on to take possession of the promised land. The wilderness, the space between Egypt and Israel, is employed to allow time to have its effects; for forty years the Israelites are required to wander, until none remain who once were slaves. Usually, time conquers space; Thomas Mann explicitly uses this notion in his rendering of the Joseph story, *Joseph and his Brothers* (1933), in which history is given a purpose and direction. Any distance can be covered, given time enough. But Moses leads his people around in circles, waiting. Time is made the victim of space; a relatively small space is expanded indefinitely until the time available to individuals is all used up.

Moses himself is punished for his own grandiosity and impatience by not being allowed to experience the fulfilment of the dream of which he is part. This is not his own dream: he is an unwilling player in something much greater than he. In some ways, it is still Joseph's dream, which does not come to an end until Joshua buries Joseph's bones in Israel; Moses is simply the major instrument through which the redemption from the nightmare takes place. More fully, it is God's dream, the dream of the unconscious – of the Other. Moses is recalcitrant, he argues with God at the moment at which he is chosen, at the site of the burning bush, but he must cooperate; something travels through him, he is a figure through which desire is expressed and achieved. Identifying with him, Freud sees his irascibility, his power and his law-giving; but he also evokes his pathos, the way his own wishes and fears have to be relinquished for his mission to be achieved.

Joseph conquers space through time; the dream that is lived out is a personal dream, but it drags his community down with it. Moses allows space to conquer time; he is part of something else, he loses his own desire through being in the grip of something more mighty and profound. One might call this the progression from the Imaginary to the Symbolic, from the assumption that mastery is possible to the awareness that it is never attainable, that dissolution beckons wherever the fantasy of wholeness is expressed. Freud articulates both elements of this progression in *The Interpretation of Dreams*: although the Imaginary fantasy of aggrandisement and conquest embodied in the Joseph identification is the dominant one, the dream of the 'promised land seen from afar' is an augur of things to come, and a chink in language revealing how possessed and uncertain is Freud himself. The dream dreams him; 'it' speaks.

Freud's identifications with Joseph and Moses involve a complex set of ambiguities surrounding time and space, subject and object, dreamer and dream. These ambiguities are closely connected with the question of mastery that pervades both this text and the wider context of psychoanalysis. Through this, too, comes the speaking voice of the unconscious and of sexual difference. Freud's explicit identifications are with male masters, heroic figures from Biblical times. Underpinning them, however, is a structure of uncertainty, whereby the hero is a disaster, or is an object in someone else's plan. No longer master of the dream, no longer able to speak and take command, this representation of masculinity is itself made problematic as something which is unstable and unclear. The dream itself takes over, with all its ambiguities and fluidity of positioning. Space and time themselves have a gender structure, which will be explored in Chapter 6; here, the lack of time and irrelevance of space in dreams, as in unconscious thought processes as a whole, emphasises the uncertainties over direction and bodily integration. If sexual difference is a primary axis around which identity is forged, the complexities of identification in *The Interpretation of Dreams* reveal the precariousness both of identity and of sexual difference itself.

THE BODY OF THE DREAM

Maintaining the Biblical imagery described above, Lacan gives the
following rule for analysis, whether of dreams or of patients:

> You must start from the text, start by treating it, as Freud does and as he
> recommends, as Holy Writ. The author, the scribe, is only a pen-pusher,
> and he comes second . . . Similarly, when it comes to our patients, please
> give more attention to the text than to the psychology of the author – the
> entire orientation of my teaching is that.
>
> (Lacan, 1954–5, p. 153)

Start with the text and assume that every element within it has significance:
this is a principle of psychoanalytic practice. In relation to the dream of
'Irma's Injection', Lacan also comments (p. 162) that 'this dream is not only
an object which Freud deciphers, it is Freud's speech' – precisely, then, the
kind of text upon which psychoanalysis operates most freely. Anzieu reads
the Irma dream even more grandiosely, as a kind of template for
psychoanalysis itself, in which can be found a crucial motivational
complex for Freud's endeavours. 'Irma's Injection' is:

> a programme dream for the whole series of subsequent discoveries that
> were to constitute psychoanalysis. It spells out the identity of both the
> body of the dream and the dream of the body. Freud experiences the
> unconscious, whose corpus he has set out to establish, as the body of the
> crime from which he must exculpate himself, for it represents sym-
> bolically, and contains metonymically, the desired body of the
> unpossessed mother.
>
> (Anzieu, 1975, p. 155)

This quotation immediately raises the issue of the status of dreams in
relation to unconscious motivations. The dream and the unconscious: the
two things are related, but not the same. Behind the dream is the
unconscious, and for Freud this is associated with the feminine principle,
the secret thing, mastery of which he craves – 'the desired body of the
unpossessed mother'. The dream is not itself unconscious, but reflects the
workings of the unconscious, it is the 'royal road' to it, the way in. It is
Irma's throat, or the woman's vagina. It is also a body of text marked by
something else, something outside the awareness of the author/dreamer,
a 'symptom' (Freud, p. 174), a text, then, like any other. The author is just
the scribe; her or his intention and personality are part of the text, not its
origin. 'The author, the scribe, is only a pen-pusher, and he comes second.'

With the dream seen as text, *The Interpretation of Dreams* becomes a
multi-levelled expression of the ambiguities of psychoanalytic thinking. At
one level is the content of each dream, as reported by Freud, ripe for
analysis by the reader. On top of that are the interpretations offered by

Freud to make sense of each of these dreams, with interpretations of these interpretations being demanded precisely by their deliberate inadequacy and incompleteness – Freud's attempt to cover his private parts. Then there is the structure of the book itself, its theoretical components and trajectory, the way it argues certain positions and occupies a rhetorical space in the great cultural debates about sexuality and the unconscious. At each of these levels the text itself is subject and object: it speaks in its own right and with its own voice, independently of Freud; but it can also be taken, operated on, thought about and discussed, made to say more than it knows.

The body of the text: subjecting the dream to scrutiny, it becomes located in the conventionally feminine position as something looked at, an object of desire. Yet, like femininity, it has its own sexuality, its own passion and life: it slips in and out of being, transgressing boundaries, ignoring formal demands, inscrutable and disruptive. It is seductive, playful and self-contradictory, attempting to subvert all attempts to control it from outside. Indeed, this makes it like psychoanalysis itself, except in its fossilised, institutional forms. It is largely this ability to express all these tensions, between knowing and being known, desiring and being desired, that makes *The Interpretation of Dreams* such a remarkably disruptive text – all its loose ends showing, but full of life.

There are a number of detailed discussions of *The Interpretation of Dreams* in the literature, the most important perhaps being Anzieu's (1975) *Freud's Self-Analysis*. Anzieu offers a primarily biographical tracing of the course of Freud's creation of psychoanalysis, using the dream book as the principal source of material for understanding Freud's unfolding concerns and ideas. In particular, he emphasises the gradual demise of Freud's relationship with Fliess, demonstrating the way several of Freud's dreams indicate an increasing distance between the two men and the development of doubts in Freud's mind about the legitimacy of Fliess' theories and behaviour. For example, on the 'non vixit' dream (Freud, pp. 548–9), Anzieu comments:

> Fliess is seriously ill: if he dies . . . Freud will be happy to have survived him . . . The person who melts away under Freud's gaze in the dream is Fliess. Freud half-recognises what Fliess has become for him – an apparition, a revenant, the ghost of John and of Julius. He is considerably embarrassed by the dream, which marks the end of his strong emotional attachment to Fliess.
>
> (Anzieu, 1975, p. 380)

If Fliess was the most significant midwife at the birth of psychoanalysis, by the end of *The Interpretation of Dreams* he is no longer needed; the baby has been born and has begun to thrive. Indeed, as will be seen below, *The Interpretation of Dreams* is in large part a working through of past identifications and dependencies, a process for Freud of divesting himself of previous affiliations to create something completely new. Whatever Fliess represented for him, and this was much, he is now liberated – at least until his next strong and destructive masculine liaison (with Jung) is formed.

While resolution of Freud's relationship with Fliess may have been a cogent precipitating motivation for much of the dreamwork recorded in the book, it is not the deepest biographical cause. The most important identification with which this text engages is that of the father. Some elements of this have already been made apparent, embedded in the figures of Joseph and Moses, and Freud himself is absolutely explicit about the significance of this strand. In the Preface to the Second Edition, he writes:

> this book has a further subjective significance for me personally – a significance which I only grasped after I had completed it. It was, I found, a portion of my own self-analysis, my reaction to my father's death – that is to say, to the most important event, the most poignant loss, of a man's life.

(Freud, p. 47)

Much of the self-justification to be found in the dreams (usually interpreted honestly and straightforwardly by Freud) is related to legitimising himself in relation to his father, even if there is often a screen of other people – colleagues and opponents – who are in the foreground. Indeed, it is a psychoanalytic platitude that dreams of rivalry and triumph can be read Oedipally as triumph over the father, and such dreams pervade the text with extraordinary regularity and ferocity. 'Uncle Josef with the Yellow Beard' (pp. 218ff) has Freud denigrating a friend in order to find a way of surpassing him professionally; the 'Botanical Monograph' 'turns out to have been in the nature of a self-justification, a plea on behalf of my own rights' (p. 259), and 'Irma's Injection' has exoneration of the self in the face of criticism and farce. In his analysis of the 'Count Thun' dream, Freud disavows the significance of his paternity, identifying the dream thought as, 'It is absurd to be proud of one's ancestry; it is better to be an ancestor oneself' (p. 564). As described earlier, again in relation to the 'Count Thun' dream, Freud recollects his father's prediction that he will 'come to nothing' and shows how his dream represents a triumph over it – not just proving the father wrong, but humiliating him as well:

> The older man (clearly my father . . .) was now micturating in front of me, just as I had in front of him in my childhood. In the reference to his glaucoma I was reminding him of the cocaine, which had helped him in the operation, as though I had in that way kept my promise. Moreover, I was making fun of him; I had to hand him the urinal because he was

blind, and I revelled in allusion to my discoveries in connection with the theory of hysteria, of which I felt so proud.

(Freud, pp. 309–10)

Most explicitly, in the context of the 'Rome' dreams, Freud recalls his father's passivity in the face of anti-semitic abuse (p. 286) and contrasts it with his own heroic identifications (although, as Anzieu points out (pp. 200–1), all the heroes documented by Freud in the commentary on the dream eventually failed to achieve their aspirations). In so doing, Freud is also asserting his own power now: in this book, he writes his success and leaves behind something permanent, including an indelible trace of his father's humiliation.

Commenting on the dream of the 'bird-beaked figures' (pp. 740–1), the last of Freud's own dreams presented in the text, Anzieu makes the following comment, linking the working-through of the relationship with the father with the production of this new 'body' of knowledge:

By placing the interpretation of the dream at the end of his book, [Freud] was confirming that he had taken back his beloved mother from his father and regained possession of her; but, more than that, he was indicating that he now had the last word on death, the last word on anxiety, the last word on separation from the primally loved object.

(Anzieu, 1975, p. 309)

The sexual curiosity so evident in the dreams, but fairly consistently and consciously suppressed by Freud in his interpretations ('It will rightly be suspected that what compels me to make this suppression is sexual material' – p. 307), comes into play as an antagonism between paternal and maternal principles, between the prohibitive presence of the father and the attainment of access to the body of the mother. This is straightforwardly Oedipal, but it is also an integrative and generative process; as dreams unfold, as the unconscious is made available for inspection, so sexuality slips into view and makes itself known. What this brings into focus is the way the disruptiveness of this text, as with many or perhaps all great works, lies in the erotisation of language which it allows to be felt.

Discussing the dream of the 'Botanical Monograph' (Freud, p. 254), Anzieu comments on its evocation of wonderment:

the wonderment of a child at the colour illustrations of a traveller's tale, the wonderment of a boy at the body of his young mother, who is as attractive as a multi-coloured picture-book, the wonderment of the male at the mystery of femaleness, and the wonderment of the connoisseur at the weaver's masterpiece.

(Anzieu, 1975, p. 293)

In every clause of this sentence, Anzieu implies that the subject is male, the object (the thing wondered at) female. Freud, too, positions the subject that same way, using 'us' to refer uncomplicatedly to males all the time.

> It is the fate of all of us, perhaps, to direct our first sexual impulse towards our mother and our first hatred and our first murderous wish against our father. Our dreams convince us that this is so.
>
> (Freud, p. 364)

Wonderment, desire and hatred: these are assumed by the male originator of the text and his male commentator to be in the province of masculinity, presumably because they are active impulses. But Freud is too honest to suppress completely the feminine identifications in which he also engages, the elements in the dreams and their interpretations that show the slippage between gender positions which is a characteristic of the unconscious. There is no knowledge of time and space in the unconscious, and in dreams these things are never fixed, but always magical and relative; so too, what seems most fixed and substantial in our identity formation is undermined as each state flows into the other, as the subject changes position with the object with no barrier in between.

The feminine identifications within *The Interpretation of Dreams* can be found in numerous places, although usually their recognition depends on agreement with the argument of some particular commentator – that is, they usually require some kind of analysis before they become apparent. For example, Resnick (1987), in an intriguing reversion to what might be called a 'pre-Freudian' account of dreams in terms of their prophetic quality, suggests that there is a 'premonitory' element in the dream of 'Irma's Injection'. In this reading, the discovery of diseased organs in Irma's mouth is to be taken not just as a symbolisation of sexuality, but as an anticipation of Freud's future illness, the cancer of the mouth that was to cause him so much agony and distort his speech. Resnick comments on Freud's search for origins and for the 'guilty' organ at the root of each illness – looking in the throat to find the source of disturbance, unravelling the symptom to find its pure cause. Then he comments, in a footnote, that Freud:

> is also looking, 'without knowing it', for an anticipated memory of his own future. 'Freud's cancer' is already speaking in the present, or in any case his worries and 'tissular' fantasies are being summoned in his transference with Irma, a transference that he was later to call 'countertransference'.
>
> (Resnick, 1987, p. 119, n. 8)

Before looking in more detail at the Irma dream, it is worth considering this point as a moment of transference or cross-sex identification. Freud looks into Irma's mouth and sees his own physical future; he sees her organ as his own. Anzieu makes a similar observation, in relation to the discovery

of a 'dull area low down on [Irma's] left', that Freud had been suffering
from heart trouble and had himself been examined for this. 'Thus the
dreamer was doubly present in his dream, both as the theoretician of the
sexual aetiology of neuroses and as a patient suffering from a possibly fatal
cardiac complaint' (Anzieu, 1975, pp. 136–7). Again, Freud slips across the
gender boundary to see himself in the woman, to feel himself the object of
concern and wonder.

This transference, as Resnick calls it, or at least this identification with
femininity, is important theoretically in psychoanalysis as it underpins the
notion of the 'negative' Oedipus complex and also shows the sustained
impact of what Freud terms 'bisexuality' past the Oedipal period and into
adulthood. Without it, too, there would be even more of a question than
there already is over the analyst's capacity to stand in as a transference
object of either sex for the patient; that is, transference depends on the
possibility of confusion and linkage across any number of structural
differences, particularly that of gender. The male analyst must be able to
take up the position of the maternal container; the female must have the
fantasised capacity to say 'no'. But there is something even more powerful
than this operating at this moment of the origin of psychoanalysis. Freud
looks around in his dreams and finds himself everywhere; as Lacan
(1954–5) notes, this is one of the major discoveries in this text. Unexpectedly, though, for one who places sexual difference at 'the bedrock' of
analysis, the point beyond which analysis cannot go, he discovers himself
in the woman as well as the man. Here he is, then, denying or transcending
difference, fascinated by it (sexually curious), but also slipping in and out
of subject positions, not allowing difference to get in the way. This is not
simply a matter of being able to understand the other; it is a process of
being, of taking on the sexual identity of the woman.

In interesting agreement with the Lacanian position on femininity,
Anzieu takes up the verbal opposites '*Auf Geseres/Auf Ungeseres*' in the 'My
son the Myops' dream (Freud, p. 572) and interprets them as an indication
of the negativity of femininity, its non-being.

> The verbal opposites . . . are determined specifically by the person to
> whom each of them is addressed – a woman in the first case, a man in
> the second. They therefore represent the difference between the sexes:
> the man is *Geseres*, in other words the cause of something imposed or
> doomed to occur (the first meaning of *Geseres*) as well as the cause of
> weeping and wailing (the second meaning of *Geseres*); the other sex is
> defined negatively, by the lack or absence (*Un-*) of the first. Freud, in his
> analysis, describes *Auf Ungeseres* as being 'quite meaningless'.
>
> (Anzieu, 1975, p. 262)

Freud rejects femininity, that much is clear. But he is also fascinated by it
and finds himself inside it, part of it. The denial of sexual difference is

closely linked up with hysteria, which in turn is a condition in which the body replaces the word, in which, therefore, the traditionally feminine sphere occludes the masculine. Freud's hysteria, the male hysteria of which he speaks in his interpretation of the dream of the 'Town Council' (p. 568), is in part his creative capacity to slip across from one subject position to the other, and find them both full of meaning. '*Ungeseres*' it may be, but not nonsense, not an empty state of existence. Looking into the mouth of the other, one finds oneself; what is taken as fixed in the position of subject or object, masculine or feminine, is again revealed in its actual instability.

THE DREAM OF IRMA'S INJECTION

It is in Freud's 'specimen dream', the dream of 'Irma's Injection', that this recurrent uncertainty over gender identity and sexual difference finds its clearest expression. Freud presents this dream and its analysis as an opportunity to demonstrate his 'method of interpretation' (p. 180), but it is clear from the detail and energy of the analysis that he is engaged in work on it for more than just pedagogic reasons. Indeed, it is in commemoration of the dreaming of this particular dream that Freud wonders to Fliess about a marble tablet being placed on the house in which he dreamt it – a tablet inscribed with the words, 'In this house, on July 24th 1895, the secret of dreams was revealed to Dr Sigm. Freud' (p. 199). A note to this effect is placed by the editors of *The Interpretation of Dreams* immediately after these last words of the chapter on Irma: 'When the work of interpretation has been completed, we perceive that a dream is the fulfilment of a wish' (pp. 198–9). Yet, as Lacan (1954–5) notes, the weight of significance placed upon this dream, and the revolutionary nature of the conclusion drawn from it, seem hardly to be linked to the manifest content of the dream interpretation itself, which has removed from it all explicit acknowledgement of its subversiveness and disturbance of sexuality. Lacan asks:

> How is it that Freud, who later on will develop the function of unconscious desire, is here content, for the first step in his demonstration, to present a dream which is entirely explained by the satisfaction of a desire which one cannot but call preconscious, and even entirely conscious?
>
> (Lacan, 1954–5, p. 151)

Lacan's own answer to this question concerns the significance of the dream analysis' revelations about the structures of ego and identity, and will be returned to below. But at a simpler level, Freud seems to be using the dream as a demonstration of his own mastery – again as an expression of his Joseph identification, but also, given the content of the dream itself, as a fantasy of sexual conquest.

Anzieu comments that the analysis of the Irma dream looks 'untidy', but in fact 'is remarkably well structured, and unfolds like a play, with the characters being introduced in the early acts and the denouement coming in the last' (1975, pp. 137–8). The play concerned is a kind of courtroom drama.

> The first act begins with a defence speech by Freud . . . and ends with his feeling afraid. In the second act, Freud stands accused by overwhelming evidence. In the third, that evidence is demolished by witnesses and lawyers. The question that lies at the heart of the tragedy, or the investigation, is now openly posed: who is responsible?
>
> (Anzieu, 1975, p. 138)

One answer to this, according to Anzieu's reading, is that the 'injection of trimethylamin' is responsible; that is, 'Irma's complaint has been caused by her frustrated sex life. It is Freud who is right, despite his detractors, when he advocates the sexual aetiology of neurosis' (p. 139). In this part of his analysis, Anzieu is thus viewing the Irma dream as part of the self-justifying tendency in *The Interpretation of Dreams*: Freud's overturning of his father's curse to discover the secret of mental life. Irma allows him to demonstrate this discovery with mastery: all those intractable females and foolish males, who between them have made a mess of things and yet stand as Freud's accusers, are despatched and Freud's own achievement is once again asserted. It is the unclean injection which is at fault, the dirty syringe; any Freudian could tell that from the material.

Freud himself gives a famous analogy to his defensiveness in the dream, with specific reference to the way the dream is structured as a formal defence plea against accusations of responsibility for Irma's disease.

> The whole plea – for the dream was nothing else – reminded one vividly of the defence put forward by the man who was charged by one of his neighbours with having given him back a borrowed kettle in a damaged condition. The defendant asserted first, that he had given it back undamaged; secondly, that the kettle had a hole in it when he borrowed it; and thirdly, that he had never borrowed a kettle from his neighbour at all.
>
> (Freud, p. 197)

Freud as interpreter of his dream can look with irony on the Freud who is the dreamer of it, revealing his foibles in the midst of his desires. But the two Freuds are not so completely divided, the analytic Freud not so much master of his procedures as he would have us believe. Anzieu (1975, p. 140) comments that 'Freud noted subsequently that thoughts which follow on from dreams are still dream-thoughts. So the thought that dreams are wish-fulfilments is an integral part of the dream content.' Analysis of the multiple-plea defence present in the dream itself (Irma herself is to blame for her pains, the pains are organic, they are to do with her widowhood, with the wrong injection, with a dirty needle) produces the generalisation that dreams are wish-fulfilments, but this too is a wish-fulfilment, the wish being that Freud should unravel the mystery of dreams. The gender structure of the dream itself magnifies this. The central object of the dream is female: Irma, with her mouth and torso open to inspection by the male subject of the dream (the dreamer) and his associates and competitors. Similarly, the dream itself is laid open for inspection and analysis by the author and psychoanalyst (the dreamer again), dreaming his way to fame on the basis of the body of this dream. The dream is thus associated with the female object, mirror reflecting mirror; analysis of the dream is analysis of the body, peering into Irma's mouth at her genital tubes. Conquering the mystery of dreams and conquering the woman; the mastery is not so mundane, not so simply a contestation of professional disdain.

Freud gives this dream to us as an illustration of his art and, by his careful ordering of the material, edits what happens, allowing the force of the dream to speak more by the centrality granted it – and by the evocativeness of the dream imagery itself – than by the comprehensiveness of the analysis. The superficial analysis given so far, however, already reveals the extent to which sexual mastery and its uncertainty pervade what is expressed in the text. Freud is explicit about suppressing sexual material that is personally revealing, but he also allows the sexuality of the dream imagery to speak clearly in the interpretation, so preserving the energy and disturbance of the dream. Freud recollects 'other medical examinations and . . . little secrets revealed in the course of them – to the satisfaction of neither party' (p. 185); he thinks of an 'intimate woman friend' of Irma's and recollects that 'I had often played with the idea that she too might ask me to relieve her of her symptoms', but 'she was recalcitrant' (ibid.); Irma's friend 'would have been wiser' than Irma, 'that is to say she would have yielded sooner. She would then have opened her mouth properly' (p. 186). Exploring the element in the dream in which an infected area on Irma's shoulder is noticed 'in spite of her dress', Freud comments 'Frankly, I had no desire to penetrate more deeply at this point' (p. 189). And, finally, there is Freud's reference to Fliess' theory about 'some very remarkable connections between the turbinal bones and the female organs of sex' (p. 194). Whatever other elements are present in the dream analysis, Freud allows it to speak in barely coded language of sexuality and domination, mostly from a straightforwardly gendered position as the 'penetrating' master, but with sufficient anxiety to allow his own feminine identification some space.

It is with the question of identification that Lacan's (1954–5) remarkable reading of the Irma dream and its interpretation deals most clearly, and it is this that enables him to show how much more radical the 'specimen' chapter is than it would have been if restricted only to the (nevertheless radical) assertion of the ubiquity of sexual desire. In this context, it is worth recalling Anzieu's comment that the dream of Irma's injection encapsulated the way 'The system of identifications that had governed [Freud] up to then crumbled away' (1975, p. 132). For Lacan as well, the dream reveals this crumbling, but not so that Freud can be reborn free of previous identifications and able to go his own way. Rather, the dream reveals the *necessary* deconstruction of the identifications which constitute the ego. It certainly deals with the shedding of identifications, with fragmentation and discursive ambiguity; but it deals with these things in order to demonstrate their centrality to the human condition.

Lacan analyses the dream in its two parts, the first being Freud's examination of Irma and the second the discussion amongst his medical colleagues – his 'congress'. Lacan's view of the ego is succinctly expressed in this Seminar.

> the ego is the sum of the identifications of the subject, with all that that implies as to its radical contingency. If you allow me to give an image of it, the ego is like the superimposition of various coats borrowed from what I will call the bric-à-brac of its props department.
>
> (1954–5, p. 155)

This is the familiar Lacanian notion of the speciousness of the ego as a unified entity: what in ordinary life we take as the core component of selfhood is revealed under analysis to be 'bric-à-brac', bits and pieces placed together or on top of one another more or less by chance, covering up an emptiness beneath. In Lacan's reading, the first section of the Irma dream, which has Freud looking deeply into Irma's mouth, brings the dreamer and the analyst face to face with the horror that lies behind this egoic surface.

Lacan states that 'The object is always more or less structured as the image of the body of the subject' (p. 167), suggesting that as Freud looks into Irma's insides so he sees his own psychic inside – a psychological rendering of the 'premonitory' sense noted by Resnick and Anzieu. What he sees there is 'something of the real, something at its most unfathomable' (*ibid.*). In fact, Lacan expresses himself exceptionally lyrically here, in a language full of the imagery of horror and dissolution. He locates the death theme in the dream through reference to the 'three women' in the first section: Irma, the ideal patient, and Freud's wife. Freud's own analysis of the three-women theme in his paper on the 'three caskets' (Freud, 1913) is, as Lacan notes, both clear and mystic: 'The last term is death, as simple as that' (Lacan, 1954–5, p. 157). Meditating on this at several points in his Seminar, Lacan produces the following encounter with what he terms 'the foundation of things, the other side of the head' (p. 154) – an encounter largely contained in one enormous sentence. The first part of the dream:

> leads to the apparition of the terrifying anxiety-provoking image, to this

real Medusa's head, to the revelation of this something which properly speaking is unnameable, the back of this throat, the complex, unlocatable form, which also makes it into the primitive subject *par excellence*, the abyss of the feminine organ from which all life emerges, this gulf of the mouth, in which everything is swallowed up, and no less the image of death in which everything comes to its end, since in relation to the illness of his daughter, which could have been fatal, there's the death of the patient whom he had lost at a time adjacent to that of the illness of his daughter, which he considered to be some mysterious sort of divine retribution for his professional negligence – *this Mathilde for that Mathilde*, he writes.

(p. 164)

The extraordinary energy and tumultuous piling-on of clauses in this passage, its hovering around loss as well as death (*'this Mathilde for that Mathilde'*), its imagery of horror, which permeates the Seminar – this is a reading resonant of the traditional but by no means trivial cultural association of feminine sexuality and death. Death comes hand-in-hand with sex, but along with this there is a parallel theme of the return to nothingness symbolised by the desire for the womb, both these elements being present in the three caskets analogy and, more formally, in Freud's (later) conceptualisation of the death drive. Reading Lacan on Freud's dream, one has the sense of the dreamer face to face with his own desire as his egoic self is discarded. Looking into the mouth of the other, into the abyss of subjectivity, what is revealed is the impossibility of the position of the conscious, integrated subject. Identifications that hold this ego in place cannot be sustained when faced with the irruption of the real. 'So this dream teaches us the following,' says Lacan (1954–5, p. 159), 'what is at stake in the function of the dream is beyond the *ego*, what in the subject is of the subject and not of the subject, that is the unconscious.'

At the moment of this encounter with the real, a second cast of characters enters the dream, this time a trio of men (Dr M., Otto, Leopold). Lacan glosses this as follows:

The relations of the subject change completely. He becomes something completely different, there's no Freud any longer, there is no longer anyone who can say *I*. This is the moment I've called the entry of the fool, since that is more or less the role of the subjects on whom Freud calls.

(*ibid.*)

But these subjects are not external to Freud: being in his dream, they are aspects of himself, they are the identifications out of which his ego is constituted. And these identifications are indeed falling apart, decomposing; the dream reveals the actual state of psychic affairs – the normal, not the pathological state. As the dream produces anxiety by revealing the fragility of the self, so 'we find ourselves present at an imaginary decomposition which is only the revelation of the normal component parts of perception' (1954–5, p. 166) – that is, so the different and unrelated elements of the supposedly integrated ego are dramatised. Freud is present in all these elements, in every member of this cast of fools hunting around for a way out of the responsibility for the horror of Irma's insides. For Lacan, it is not the content of the discourse thus produced which matters, but the presence of these imaginary elements of the ego and the way they disappear to reveal behind them something more powerful and insidious, a name that, despite being completely inscrutable, fixes the whole symbolic pattern into place.

Freud's report of his dream culminates in his vision of the formula for trimethylamin ($N–CH_3/CH_3/CH_3$) and his comment about the syringe not being clean. Lacan takes this formula and addresses it as an inscription of 'another voice', something which just appears written in the air, without an agency behind it – what he refers to, again with Biblical allusiveness, as its *'Mene, Mene, Tekel, Upharsin* aspect' (p. 158). This formula, of no significance in what it says, is of ultimate significance because of its act of speaking; it is thus that it reveals to the dreamer what is at the heart of the dream. Here is Lacan's full exposition of this point:

> In the dream of Irma's injection, it is just when the world of the dreamer is plunged into the greatest imaginary chaos that discourse enters into play, discourse as such, independently of its meaning, since it is a senseless discourse. It then seems that the subject decomposes and disappears. In the dream there's the recognition of the fundamentally acephalic character of the subject, beyond a given point. The point is designated by the N of the trimethylamin formula. That's where the *I* of the subject is at that moment . . . Just when the hydra has lost its heads, a voice which is nothing more than *the voice of no-one* causes the trimethylamin formula to emerge, as the last word on the matter, the word for everything. And this word means nothing except that it is a word.
>
> (Lacan, 1954–5, p. 170)

Whether this version of the Irma dream is produced to be in line with Lacan's already existing theory, or whether the theory follows from the analysis, is an interesting point but not one that is crucial here. Certainly, Lacan's reading is different from Freud's, and not just because Freud suppresses material that reveals too much about his person. Nevertheless, Lacan's meditation on Freud's meditation on Freud's dream of Irma expresses a dream of its own, a vision of what it means to be a dreamer and a creator. 'It is not me', is what Lacan understands Freud to be saying: 'It is my unconscious, it is this voice which speaks in me, beyond me' (1954–5, p. 171). As the ego dissolves, there is a symmetrical relationship between the three women of the first part of the dream and the three men of the second part. Freud, the dreamer, stands outside them all, but by the very nature of things he embodies them all – they are all aspects of his own imagination, creatures of his dream. Typically, he looks into the throat of the woman to find horror and dissolution; he looks to the babble of the men for consolation and connivance at a relinquishment of responsibility for the destruction he has wrought. But as the ego dissolves and the identifications out of which it is built are revealed to be no more than superficial allegiances, so a more truthful formula is revealed, something which is sexual but not in itself sexed. Freud's dream encompasses death and otherness, making them available to the consciousness of the dreamer and analyst. They are also available to the dreamers and analysts who follow, who can see Freud's unconscious at work. The dream thus demonstrates Freud's art and some of the truth of his theory, but not through his mastery, rather through the activity of his unconscious.

In this reading, sexual difference becomes less fixed than ever. At first sight, the dream of Irma's injection is a paradigmatically masculine account of penetration and domination. Repelled by the woman's intransigence, the man forces himself upon her, causing her nothing but suffering and at the same time fantasising about the perfect woman who is just out of reach. Then a cast of portentous fools, other men, is called in to play a game of shifting the blame around, exculpating the dreamer from responsibility for the woman's distress. It is all right; it was broken in the first place; it is someone else's fault. What could be more gendered than this? However, reading the dream and its interpretation more fully, there is a series of identifications at work which conventionally would be associated with both femininity and masculinity: Freud can take both subject positions, he is the nodal point (the 'N'), with female and male caskets branching out from him, but he is not completely expressed by either. The bisexuality of this is also quite conventional, though an advance on the stereotypy of the previous account. Now Freud, male dreamer though he is, reveals a capacity for both masculine and feminine attributes; he can put himself in the shoes of either, and understand what each has to say.

Lacan's reading goes even further than this 'bisexuality', however. There is still a representational dynamic around sexual difference: the unconscious speaks of horror and death through immersion in the woman, the other side of the skin. This losing of self and identity, this castration, is a conventional element in Lacanian imagery (and in some post-Lacanian work, particularly that of Kristeva, 1980) and it is always expressed through the medium of the feminine 'Other', that which is excluded from the discourse of the Symbolic. But in the analysis of the dream of Irma's injection, Lacan shows how rich an understanding of desire and loss can be built up from this apparently traditional and perhaps sterile or even misogynistic sexual differentiation, and how this can disrupt any fixed position on difference itself. As the identifications which constitute the ego dissolve, the subject is left referring to something other than what it experiences itself to be, something that writes the formula for it. This something is not in itself gendered; it is too impersonal for that. Speaking for the subject, it muddles up 'subject' positions, mixing what is one with what is other, subject and object. This does not dispense with sexual difference, but it interrogates it impersonally, without formal allegiance. There is this 'masculine' and this 'feminine', but the subject is other than these categories; inserted into them, for sure, but nevertheless outside what they have to say. The social categories of gender are germane to the identifications of the ego; but behind the ego is something else, visible when one can look without blinking or turning aside. In this reading, Freud's 'self-analysis' is genuinely heroic: the analytic gaze that challenges all of us to see more than we can usually see.

DISRUPTION AND THE DREAM

The Interpretation of Dreams is a text marked by Freud's presence at numerous levels and in different positions: as author and subject, as analyst and subject, as dreamer and subject, and as author, analyst, dreamer and object. It is a text dedicated to mastery, in which Freud displays a virtuoso command of the principles of dream interpretation, thus banishing the secrets of the night as well as the doubts of his adversaries. Freud as master is competing against others: the body of knowledge lies there to be uncovered, it is an aspect of nature, something which has eluded Freud's predecessors because of its uncanniness and obscurity – its relationship to the 'dark continent' – but something which is nevertheless a material entity, available to the activities of reason and analysis. Indeed, as psychoanalysis is in general concerned with the colonisation of the irrational and its subjugation by the forces of reason and science, in this specific instance it is also dedicated to reducing the area of recalcitrance in nature, making the world more predictable and secure.

The traditional sexuality of this description is quite transparent. The obscure is the feminine – nature, the night, the dark continent, the dream. Masculinity is identified with rationality, with mastery of this obscurity, with light in the darkness, with the triumph of science over nature. It is characterised by self-aggrandisement, an economy of competition: Freud explicitly builds his dream book on rivalry with others which in turn derives from his need to overcome his father's disparagement of him. Nature is therefore being attacked for the sake of a strengthened position in the world of men, in just the same way as adolescent male sexuality has more to do with establishing one's masculine status than with desire for the other (Seidler, 1985). But nature is also being attacked for its own sake, as an ambivalent object of desire. The boy's 'epistemologic impulse' is conventionally ascribed by psychoanalysts to curiosity about the mother's body: a wish to know it and understand its secrets, but also to act upon it, to take revenge on it for the terrifying dependency characteristic of early infancy, as well as for the abandonment experienced as the mother pushes the child away. The subtleties and unpredictability of the maternal body, the reminiscence of its smell and feel, provide an underpinning for the desire to know and conquer nature, linking with all those mind/body, reason/nature, sanity/insanity dichotomies so familiar in all parts of the social world.

In this scheme of things, the dream is the object of psychoanalytic enquiry, hence feminine in tone. Mysterious and obscure, a creature of the night, the dream is laid open on the table, dissected and inspected, penetrated with the rational zeal of the Freudian discoverer. Understanding dreams gives power in the world of men (Joseph); however, it also makes the night less fearsome – it is a way of articulating and dealing with inner horror, repudiated but deeply felt. Interpreting dreams is thus in truth an act of mastery, but it betrays its own dynamic uncertainty. Throughout this chapter, it has been stressed that Freud's own articulation of dream analysis in *The Interpretation of Dreams* is shot through with ambivalence and with the voice of unconscious desire. This voice speaks in his place, showing how his personal identifications slip between those which might be characterised as masculine and those which might be feminine, always searching. The act of writing up the dreams and presenting their analysis to the world, a triumphant act of mastery, is also one in which the irrational is allowed its say, and Freud's own conflict-filled personality is offered up for inspection. Subject and object then shift again: Freud on the table, being examined, the feminine object of masculine desire.

All this applies too to psychoanalysis in general. It often speaks in a voice full of authority and certainty; but when it comes down to it, it never knows what position it is in. Trading in the mysteries of the night, it will always flounder; giving irrationality its voice, it will never be completely rational. If psychoanalysis is an expressive discourse, what it expresses will always include the unconscious – both subject and object of the psychoanalytic enterprise, both 'masculine' and 'feminine' of the sexual divide. Far from sexual difference being something fixed and absolute, the bedrock against which analysis stops in wonder, it comes to look more like a mist – and perhaps one can walk right through.

NOTE

1   Unless specifically noted, all references to Freud's writing in this chapter are to Freud, 1900, *The Interpretation of Dreams*, published as volume 4 in the Pelican Freud Library (Harmondsworth: Penguin, 1976).

Chapter 4

Masculine mastery and fantasy, or the meaning of the phallus

The ambiguities of sexual difference revolve around uncertainty over the content and fixedness of the categories 'masculine' and 'feminine'. Within psychoanalysis, this is expressed by a fascination with gender divergence which has been characteristic of psychoanalytic theory since its inception, accompanied by a playful and ambivalent tradition of transgression. In the context of the transference, the analyst, whether male or female, can be related to as either masculine or feminine, whether in terms of 'whole object' identity (as mother or father), or part-object attribute (breast, penis), and therefore has to have the capacity to tolerate this boundary confusion if the projections of the patient are to be understood and ameliorated. For analysands, crossing conventional gender boundaries, particularly in terms of sexual object choice, is a common phenomenon; psychoanalysis is explicit about the significance of such homoeroticism and 'bisexuality', theorised primarily in terms of sexually charged aspects of gender identity. At a more general and theoretical level, psychoanalysis struggles to find its place amongst categories which traditionally reduce to a masculine/feminine dimorphism: rational and irrational, reason and emotion, science and art, culture and nature. In the end, as described in the previous chapter when discussing Freud's work, it becomes clear that psychoanalysis plays out both the central subjective significance of sexual division (that one experiences oneself as masculine or feminine in ways which are emotionally highly charged) and its untenability (that, because masculine and feminine are constructed categories, they never hold firm, but are always collapsing into one another). Moreover, because of the centrality of sexuality in psychoanalysis, the ambiguity of sexual difference comes to infiltrate all its domains.

Amongst psychoanalysts of the post-Freudian era, it is Lacan who has produced most outrage and energy in discussions of sexual difference, and who seems to have most self-consciously played with the divisions, appearing both to assert the ubiquity of sexual difference and to undermine it in theory and in practice. It is perhaps no surprise that an industry of competing authorities on Lacan has grown up, especially given the difficulty of his work and its availability to a range of alternative constructions. Lacan himself talks authoritatively, as if he is absolutely certain about the truth of what he says. Indeed, in a lecture given on television that supposedly offered an introduction to psychoanalysis to a mass audience, but which in fact made no concessions of any kind towards ease of understanding, Lacan claimed, 'I always speak the truth'. The irony here is so obvious that one must assume it to be intentional, because the content of Lacanian theory seems on the face of it to be opposed to any claim that anyone can 'speak the truth' – can have a complete grasp of what is real. Authoritatively, speaking as a famous psychoanalyst who is in possession of a knowledge so deep that it cannot easily be communicated, Lacan tells us that there is no absolute authority, that the belief that anyone – any 'Other' – can hold all the answers to our questions, is an illusion. There is a law, it fixes us in the Symbolic order, but try to master it and all one discovers is that no-one is master, no-one is an absolute authority; the one 'supposed' to know does not 'really' know at all.

This can be restated more strongly and personally. Lacan's absolute certainty, his wilfulness and capriciousness, his adoption of a god-like voice, his dismissal of opponents and acolytes alike, his assumption of the right to bend the rules of analysis, all these are the most infuriating evidence of mastery. This authority, however, is used to promulgate a theory attesting to the *impossibility* of authority: no-one can be master of the unconscious. Moreover, Lacan claims to let his unconscious do the work, so that when he speaks he is evoking the experience of analysis as well as discoursing upon it. The unconscious speaks for him, in very public circumstances; but by doing this it acts in 'his' service – Lacan uses his own unconscious as part of his performance. Using it, however, it ceases to be unconscious in the simple psychoanalytic sense of something unavailable to conscious control and manipulation. Thus, in order to demonstrate that no-one can master the unconscious, Lacan becomes its master.

The paradoxes of authority and power which are expressed in the form and content of Lacanian theory should not be regarded as some extraneous obstacle to understanding. Rather, these paradoxes go to the heart of the question that underpins any causal account of sexual difference: what is it that produces sexual difference and fixes the relationship between the sexes so that gender dimorphism comes to be experienced as an asymmetrical and unequivocal fact of existence? For Lacan, this question is best formulated as the question of the 'meaning of the phallus', that which is taken to be the sign of difference, privileging one sex over the other, producing divergent subjectivities. As will be described more fully below, the phallus in this theory is both something which symbolises power and something which is empty of content, precisely paralleling the paradoxes of authority and mastery – and these paradoxes are once again enacted in the structure of the theory itself. Desiring to understand Lacan is like wanting to have the phallus; the fantasy is that it would bring in its wake everything connected with power and authority, because that is what it represents and seems to be. But just as the idea that one can own the phallus is an imaginary illusion, part of what Lacan terms the Imaginary, so is the fantasy of what conquering Lacan might achieve.

It is, of course, possible that the lure of Lacan's work lies in its obscurity, that behind the veil of difficult language there is nothing of substance. If this were so, it would make his writing a kind of masquerade, something eliciting the desire to possess (understand) by virtue of its inscrutability. It would be only because its meaning (or lack of it) is so playfully veiled that it is arousing and desirable; remove the veils and the mystery goes. Under these conditions, Lacan's reputation relies on intimidation: if people were only more willing to challenge the difficulty of his writing, they would see how apt the 'emperor's new clothes' accusation often applied to him is; once the pretence is seen through, nothing remains. The irony here, however, is that this is very much what Lacan says about desire itself, and in a different way about the pursuit of femininity as other to the male: that these enterprises refer to empty sets, that the pursuit is all there is. As the object of our desire slips away and is more and more elusive, so we desire to have it, to master it all the more.

Here, therefore, is more evidence of how one can fall into the grip of this master of manipulation and paradox. If the only thing that is interesting about Lacan's writing is its obscurity, and if behind this obscurity it is actually devoid of meaningful content, then it functions as a demonstration of the Lacanian theory of desire, so it cannot just be empty after all. Lacan wins either way: either his writing, difficult though it might be, denotes a specific theory or set of theories with which we might want or have to grapple; or its difficulty is its way of connoting the same theories, of expressing their truth in the practice of speaking and writing. In psychoanalytic thought, symptoms express something about the nature of the underlying forces from which they arise. Lacan's writing may be a kind of symptomatic enactment of his theory of the phallus; and also of the feminine object of desire.

Many people have noted Lacan's fascination and identification with femininity, his constant playing to the ladies. Clément (1983, p. 61) comments, 'the whole cast of characters in his early work consists of women. Not a single man is present . . . Here is a man whose thinking is founded entirely on the study of female paranoia. A man who never stopped talking about women.' Lacan claims to know more about women than women do themselves; but he also takes on feminine poses as the performer, the hard to find, the one engaging in masquerade. Identifying himself as an hysteric, he claims to know both woman and man inside out – or at least, as in the following quotation, he can be read by others as making that claim:

The male analyst understands the woman and speaks in her place, is the perfection of the hysteric, no symptoms, save only mistakes in gender, the misidentifications indeed, running in and out of her from *his* position, miss-taken but perfect – fear, desire, the love letter as grounding of authority.

(Heath, 1987, p. 7)

Lacan's mastery of the unconscious is what is on display, but the unconscious is also that which eludes mastery, that which is multifarious and seductive, playful and contradictory. In conventional gender terms, it lies on the feminine pole, and all its associations are feminine in tone (see Chapter 2). Lacan is the master, his texts are impossible yet true. Lacan is also the one pored over, taken apart, to be desired and if possible owned, and even perhaps loved.

Reading Lacan on sexual difference can be seen to be intolerable, but unavoidable if one is to grasp the tension produced by this topic within psychoanalysis. His texts, in translation (masked) perhaps even more than in the original (masked one layer less), enact the whole problem of authority, mastery and control just as they discuss it in their content. They lay down the law and yet they play on their seductiveness; the seduction is a major element in the mastery. As part of this game, sexuality is embodied in Lacan's language, particularly in its mysteriousness; and alongside sexuality, inextricably part of it, comes sexual difference as it is played out through the dialectic of mastery and subversion that permeates Lacan's work. But sexual difference is not just implicit here, it is explicitly theorised through the Lacanian conception of the phallus, and in the account this produces of the differing positions with respect to the phallus taken up by males and females.

PHALLOCENTRIC THEORY

The Lacanian phallus has been the focus of much critical scrutiny and controversy. It has, it seems, at least one meaning; or perhaps it just, like the thing itself, signifies to excess. What is the meaning of the phallus? As 'The Meaning of the Phallus', it is the translation by Jacqueline Rose of a paper by Lacan, a paper which is worth taking extremely seriously as a possible source of material for unpacking the Lacanian conundrum.

In their introduction to 'The Meaning of the Phallus' (Lacan, 1958[1]), Mitchell and Rose (1982) write that it is 'Lacan's most direct exposition of the status of the phallus in the psychoanalytic account of sexuality' (p. 74). They continue:

This is perhaps the article which illustrates most clearly the problem of giving an explanation of the phallus which avoids reducing it to the biological difference between the sexes, but which none the less tries to provide a differential account, for men and for women, of its effects.

(Lacan, p. 74)

In 'The Meaning of the Phallus', Lacan himself locates his work on the theory of the phallus in the historical context of psychoanalytic debate on the nature and origins of femininity. One of the things that attracts him to this debate is its 'passion' (p. 77), specifically the 'passion for doctrine' to be found in the early debates on the phallic phase. Here, 'passion' is being used in the straightforward sense of 'enthusiasm' and is employed in order to contrast the energy of that phase of psychoanalysis – its own 'phallic phase' in which the question of sexual difference is unavoidably posed – with the withering away of this energy and personal investment to be found in later developments. Lacan is 'nostalgic' for this passion particularly in the light of 'the degradation of psychoanalysis consequent on its American transplantation' (ibid.); following the early debates there has been a period in which nothing seems to have been achieved.

It is tempting to see this in developmental terms. The early debates were psychoanalysis' phallic phase, struggling with incestuous wishes until castration anxiety became too great and repression intervened, with the questions of the phallus and of sexual difference left unresolved while analysts got on with the latency task of adapting (passionlessly) to the outside world. Lacan pays tribute to the diversity of positions taken up during this phase, and even acknowledges the worth of some of the contributions, although he also declares that the apparent closure produced at the end of the debate was a false one, a covering over of a problem that 'refuses to go away'. All the previous contributions had juvenile elements in them, shown for example in Ernest Jones' work as fantasies of 'natural rights' and of the maternal body. Now, however, Lacan is here to 're-open the question' (p. 78). With the benefit of post-Freudian linguistics, something perhaps learnt during latency, Lacan can promote and face the full (genital) passion of sexuality; it is in the maturity of Lacanian thought that the early debates find their fulfilment. 'The Meaning of the Phallus' is the moment when passion returns, when it becomes possible to think again about sex and to face the pain as well as the excitement of sexual difference. This might also explain the element of romance which runs through the paper, its unabashed concern not just with desire, but with love. Lacan is never too much at home with humility, and here as elsewhere he takes on the burden of the whole future of psychoanalysis; he sees himself as its next important stage.

'Passion', however, is a word with a complex range of associations in 'The Meaning of the Phallus'. Shortly after its first use, it recurs to indicate something of the fusional force with which the unconscious operates. Translating Freud's vision of an unconscious full of physical energy into linguistic terms, Lacan manages to convey both a sexual and a religious impulse in one romantic image.

It is Freud's discovery that gives to the opposition of signifier to signified the full weight which it should imply: namely, that the signifier has an active function in determining the effects in which the signifiable appears as submitting to its mark, becoming through that passion the signified.

(Lacan, p. 78)

And then, immediately:

This passion of the signifier then becomes a new dimension of the human condition, in that it is not only man who speaks, but in man and through man that it speaks, that his nature is woven by effects in which we can find the structure of language, whose material he becomes.

(*ibid.*)

Whose passion, or the passion of what psychic elements, is at stake in these extracts? In the first, the sense is at least ambiguous: it may be that the passion referred to is that of the 'signifiable' as it becomes the signified, or perhaps 'that passion' refers back to the 'active function' of the signifier. The second extract is clearer, the passion belongs to the signifier; but it is now not so much a process as something that 'becomes a dimension', or perhaps a phenomenon – the way in which human subjects are 'woven by effects' in which language inheres. These are the effects of the play of combination and substitution, along 'the two axes of metaphor and metonymy which generate the signified' (p. 79), and these effects are 'determinant in the institution of the subject'. The 'passion of the signifier', then, has become that which forms the human subject; something both creative and coercive in form.

Unpacking all this is no easy task, even ignoring the exigencies of translation of Lacan's dense prose. From a position in which the signifier 'passion' seemed to refer unproblematically to sexual energy, it has become imbued with the notion both of active force and of bowing to something, of a certain transportation of subjectivity in which agency is given up and made subject to something else. This is akin to the religious sense of 'passion', the process whereby one succumbs to the Other, to that 'dimension of the human condition' in which one is a tool and not a subject, in which the Other speaks in one's place. In Lacan's thought, this is a process that refers to the Oedipus complex read as a formal structure of language. The apparently speaking subject is actually only able to speak by being itself positioned in a pre-existing linguistic order. The subject is thus always speaking in relation to something outside itself, some third term or 'Law'. Here Lacan's immersion in phallocentrism is made explicit: this third term/law is the one to be found in the Oedipal triangle, the paternal metaphor or 'Name of the Father'. It is in relation to this masculine term that the child becomes a speaking subject, it is in relation to it that signification continues to operate, and it is also in relation to this term that the process of analysis occurs.

To repeat an example given in Chapter 2, the following passage from Felman shows both the strength and weakness of the Lacanian claim here.

The psychoanalytic narrative is nothing other, for Lacan, than the story of, precisely, the discovery of the third participant in the structure of the dialogue. And this dramatic, narrative and structural discovery implicitly refers to Oedipus.

(Felman, 1987, p. 127)

Felman states that, in analysis, the analyst searches to uncover the way in which the masculinised speaking other is at work in the discourse of the analysand. But the emphatic terms 'nothing other' and 'precisely' are disturbing here. If one were a psychoanalyst, one could read Felman's emphasis as indicating uncertainty: why does she need so to italicise, so firmly to rule out alternatives? Why cannot the psychoanalytic narrative be 'both ... and', rather than 'nothing other' than something absolutely precise, the discovery of the Oedipal third term? Writing from the position of the woman disciple of Lacan, Felman expresses with great emphasis the narrowest possible masculine rendering of the analytic experience. Analysis is about finding one's place in the Law. Yet something else seems to speak in her sentences, presumably unconsciously intended, drawing attention to this narrowness. As it speaks, her discourse adopts the defence of reaction formation, stating the narrow position more firmly, but in so doing it draws attention to its own ambivalence. The analyst's task is to find the Law for the patient, but it is also the analyst's task to question that Law and all that it fixes in place.

'Passion', then, has become the activity of the signifier and the submission of the signified, the force of the speaker and the subjugation of the spoken. It is a word containing tremendous tension: it is a full word; in Lacanian jargon, one is tempted to say it is a word that enacts 'jouissance'. But despite the potential feminine energy that this suggests, and despite the passionate debate from which this all stems being that concerning feminine sexuality, the 'dimension' this passion refers to is a masculinised one, a phallocentric fascination with the Symbolic order. As will be described below, there is rather a strong tendency for this particular trajectory to be played out in 'The Meaning of the Phallus': that the feminine is seen as full of subversive energy and excitement, but as having no agency and nothing to say. The feminine is there, but mainly as a query, an indication that all is not quite right with the world. It slumbers, speaking only as something which is absent. Grosz (1990, p. 146) complains, 'If Lacan begs women to tell him in what their pleasure consists, he is not prepared to hear what they have to say'. Moore perhaps grasps more clearly the colonisation going on here, the sense of Lacan as trickster and fraud.

In deciphering the language of the 'other' and then claiming it for themselves, these theoretical drag queens don the trappings of femininity for a night on the town without so much as a glance back at the poor woman whose clothes they have stolen.

(Moore, 1988, p. 185)

The energy of femininity, fantasised as passionate and full, becomes another element in the Lacanian masquerade, as the full weight of phallic mastery is brought into play.

It is worth considering the nature of this mastery a little further. Lacan emphasises the way paternity operates linguistically, through the Name of the Father and the prohibition its enunciation brings in its wake. In this, he is working in the Biblical tradition in which the Name of God is generally left unspoken, because of its terrible power. In the traditional Judaic ritual, it was only on the highest of holy days and after an enormous effort of study and purification that the High Priest was allowed into the holiest part of the Temple to speak this Name and to use it both to expunge the sin of the people and to commit them further to the Law. Speaking the symbol of the highest power calls into being that power, with potentially savage effects should anything go wrong. In this tradition, the effect of speech is so potent that it dominates the material world: pronouncing the Name is to enter into the mystery.

Freud, in his own way, writes from within this tradition, particularly in relation to gender. In 'Moses and Monotheism', which is ostensibly an attempt to historicise the Biblical figure of Moses, Freud offers an ironic and misogynistically reductionist rendering of the relationship between mastery and the symbolic, devoid of its sacred elements but nonetheless committed to the cultural superiority of language over the body. Discussing the supposed historical transition from matriarchy to patriarchy, he comments:

But this turning from the mother to the father points in addition to a victory of intellectuality over sensuality – that is, an advance in civilisation, since maternity is proved by the evidence of the senses while paternity is a hypothesis, based on an inference and a premise. Taking sides in this way with a thought process in preference to a sense perception has proved to be a momentous step.

(Freud, 1939, p. 361)

Explicit in this quotation is an identification of the masculine (the father) with the symbolic ('intellectuality') and the feminine with the body ('sensuality'). The former is victorious over the latter: the 'thought process' subjugates the sense. Similarly, it is by the paternal name that children are known; it is the man's name that counts. Of course, the irony here is that proof of paternity does not just require 'an inference and a premise'; it relies on the *word* of the woman – something which, in Lacanian thought, is bound to be unreliable – and, in disputed cases nowadays, on a very material genetic test.

For Lacan, as one might expect, the workings of the word are more obscure yet also more subtly controlling. It is a matter of being spoken by something absolute and also mysterious – something which, if it were not for Lacan's relentless opposition to all imaginary wholes, might again be termed religious.

> It speaks in the Other, I say, designating by this Other the very place called upon by a recourse to speech in any relation where it intervenes. If it speaks in the Other, whether or not the subject hears it with his own ears, it is because it is there that the subject, according to a logic prior to any awakening of the signified, finds his signifying place.
>
> (Lacan, p. 79)

The idea that 'it' speaking is a reference to the unconscious and, through this, to something experienced as alien to the subject yet determinant of the subject's being has become a familiar one in Lacan's work. The quotation continues:

> The discovery of what he articulates in that place, that is, in the unconscious, enables us to grasp the price of the division (*Spaltung*) through which he is thus constituted.
>
> (*ibid.*)

The 'Other' and the 'unconscious' are being run together here, partially differentiated from one another but both employed to communicate the idea of something outside and yet within the subject, something causal and yet somehow not owned. 'It', 'the Other', 'the unconscious': the impact of this progression is one of impersonal alienation, something abstract and impoverished, yet troubling too. Lacan chooses what are in some respects the emptiest possible terms to communicate the force of the 'division' introduced into subjectivity by language. As we speak, so we are spoken. Put crudely, language seems to speakers to be something which is used to express thoughts, yet its intractability, and the *failures* of communication which so characterise speech and writing, reveal that language has a life and project of its own, that it operates as a division within and between people more than as a link. In developmental terms, this division occurs at various points, but most firmly at the time of the Oedipal negation of incestuous wishes. This moment marks the entry into the subject of a repressive paternal order, making the subject 'subject to' a set of prohibitions summarisable as 'No, you may not go there'.

Given the Lacanian emphasis on the masculinity of language, its absorption in the paternal Symbolic, what appears out of the mist here is an image of a domineering patriarchal structure which is both impersonal and at the heart of subjecthood. The subject is 'constituted' by division, and this division is accessed through exploration of 'what he articulates' in the unconscious, which in turn reflects a nature 'woven by effects in which we can find the structure of language' (Lacan, p. 78). Mastery, then, is the province of the word. And this is a curiously ambiguous phenomenon. Mastery is both deathly and creative: the former because it is constituted as a prohibition – the paternal 'No' – that limits what is allowable to the subject; and the latter because it sets in motion an order of things – the Symbolic order – without which there would be no communication (or miscommunication), no culture and no social organisation. The pursuit of mastery may be a journey in pursuit of an (Imaginary) mirage; but there is a lot of fun to be had on the way, as Lacan himself enacts. This is the master's word in action: as Lacan speaks, so the dead hand of orthodoxy reaches out to stifle dissent; but he also provides some tools to see through the fraud as well.

PHALLIC FUNCTIONS; OR, HOW MEN AND WOMEN FIND OUT WHO THEY ARE

Mastery, paternity, prohibition, 'it' speaking: Lacan has set the scene for a formal reconsideration of the phallic phase. The next sentence in 'The Meaning of the Phallus' following the discussion of language and the Other, is 'The phallus is elucidated in its function here' (Lacan, p. 79). All this speaking about otherness, then, leads to the meaning of the phallus, or at least to its function, and Lacan seems to be promising to deal fully and finally with the phallus itself, signifier of signifiers, something ultimate and profound. Unfortunately, however, but perhaps predictably, uncovering the phallus turns out to be not such an easy process.

Lacan makes a number of statements in 'The Meaning of the Phallus' which have the structure 'the phallus is . . .', but at first glance none of them seems to lead anywhere further than the notion that the phallus is 'a signifier', which it could hardly fail to be. Here is a selection:

> the phallus is not a fantasy, if what is understood by that is an imaginary effect. Nor is it as such an object (part, internal, good, bad, etc. . . .) in so far as this term tends to accentuate the reality involved in a relationship. It is even less the organ, penis or clitoris, which it symbolises.
>
> (Lacan, p. 79)

> the phallus is a signifier, a signifier whose function in the intrasubjective economy of analysis might lift the veil from that which it served in the mysteries. For it is to this signifier that it is given to designate as a whole the effect of there being a signified, inasmuch as it conditions any such effect by its presence as signifier.
>
> (ibid., pp. 79–80)

The phallus is the privileged signifier of that mark where the share of the logos is wedded to the advent of desire.

(Lacan, p. 82)

The phallus is the signifier of this *Aufhebung* itself which it inaugurates (initiates) by its own disappearance.

(*ibid.*, p. 82)

Considering these extracts a little more fully, however, they do begin to offer a way forward. The Lacanian phallus is neither a physical organ nor a specific fantasy, but it is a signifier with a particular function: it 'designates as a whole the effect of there being a signified'; moreover, it has a 'privileged' relationship with the 'wedding' of 'the logos' and 'the advent of desire'. It is thus generative and connecting, possessed, as one might imagine, of an aura of procreation and sexual linkage. On the other hand, it also specifically signifies an '*Aufhebung*', a cancellation – it is, therefore, not to be thought of as something positive and full of potency, but as a kind of negativity which disappears if it is held up to the light. It is in this negativity that may be found the one real definition of the phallus offered by 'The Meaning of the Phallus', a definition phrased in terms of the necessary conditions for the phallus to work.

[The] phallus can only play its role as veiled, that is, as in itself the sign of the latency with which everything is struck as soon as it is raised to the function of signifier.

(*ibid.*, p. 82)

The positioning of this sentence is as a response to a series of possible answers (with the structure, 'One might say . . .') to the question of why it is the phallus that should be the 'privileged signifier'. These answers are, for instance, connected with the 'turgidity' of the phallus or (relatedly) to its appearance as something which 'stands out as most easily seized upon in the real of sexual copulation' – a formulation which seems rather concrete and exact, expressing both the phallus' power and its vulnerability. Lacan, however, says that these explanations are 'veils', and what they veil is the way the phallus itself only operates as veiled; perhaps this makes the explanations themselves too phallic, referring back to the literal-mindedness of the phallic stage of development. Prior to Lacan, no-one has understood that the phallus cannot be taken literally, as something to be grabbed and pulled upon. It only works if it is not seen, its message being that there is no centre to power, just the emanation of some remarkable effects. The phallus is a function, something that happens and makes things happen; it is often related to as a fantasy, like the fantasy of mastery, but no-one can have it because it is not a thing to be had.

There is a considerable amount of romance and mystery in this: something operates in the world which is immensely powerful, has effects felt everywhere, and yet can never be uncovered or known. Patriarchal emblems other than the phallus itself, particularly religious emblems, have shared these characteristics: a mystery at the heart of the human soul, both core to human life and yet always finally unknowable. Lacan continually asserts the phallus' status as signifier, as something without specific content yet with powerful effects that are sufficient to generate meanings. Amongst commentators on Lacan, there has been some attempt to understand this in ways which make it possible to free the phallus from its patriarchal context. For example, in Bowie's (1991, p. 128) gloss, 'The phallus is the promise of meaning organised by an organ and, equally, it is the loss or cancellation of meaning perpetually being foretold.' Moreover:

> the phallus is entitled to its extraordinary structuring and dialecticising role only if it is thought of as un-male, in a terrain that both sexes inhabit and a pivotal point for their countless mutual determinations.
>
> (Bowie, 1991, p. 145)

Ragland-Sullivan (1991, p. 61) also claims a non-gendered position for the phallus by asserting that the penis is only one symbol of it. 'Other symbols of the (imaginary) phallus', she writes, 'are the breast, the voice, the gaze, fragments and slits of the body, scents, and so on' – a series of feminine associations to cover over (veil?) the primary masculine one. To say that the phallus is the signifier generating the effects of meaning is therefore not necessarily a gendered statement. On the other hand, if the phallus is disconnected from its referent, it becomes the kind of fetishised ideal object which Lacanian theory is supposedly against. Gallop (1988, p. 128) comments, 'One of the weaknesses of the Lacanian orthodoxy is to render *phallus* transcendental, not dependent on the penis and its contingencies.' There seems no getting away from it: whatever veils are used, the phallus is surely a male symbol, built on the anatomical model of the penis and operating as a powerful – the primary – signifier in the lexicon of the unconscious. Despite the protestations, the injunctions not to confuse the phallus with the penis, this discourse has its roots and its emblems in masculinity. What we have here is a sexed distribution of signs, in which subjectivity is produced around a sexual divide.

The phallus cannot be known directly, it speaks its name only through its effects. And the primary function of these effects is to produce human subjects who are sexed in their essence – who are generated along a sexual divide. So the phallus is an abstract signifier and is decidedly not the penis, yet it effects a split resulting in masculinity and femininity as attributes and subjective states, each with a different relationship to the phallus itself. Put simply, masculinity and femininity are organised differently in relation to the phallus, something which comes as no surprise.

Lacan seems contradictory here. Clinical facts, he says, 'go to show that the relation of the subject to the phallus is set up regardless of the anatomical difference between the sexes' (p. 76). In particular, Lacan refers to Freud's notion that in the phallic phase of development the clitoris is 'raised to the function of the phallus' for the girl, apparently meaning that there is no difference in gendered experience until the Oedipus complex is dissolved. But he also notes (p. 83) that 'simply by keeping to the function of the phallus, we can pinpoint the structures which will govern the relations between the sexes'. The 'elucidation' of the phallus' function thus needs to be explored further, if sexual difference is to be clearly located.

Lacan identifies the differing relationship of men and women to the phallus in a relatively simple dichotomy.

> Let us say that these relations will revolve around a being and a having which, because they refer to a signifier, the phallus, have the contradictory effect of on the one hand lending reality to the subject in that signifier, and on the other making unreal that to be signified.
>
> (Lacan, pp. 83–4)

There is a good deal packed into this apparently nonchalant 'Let us say', particularly with reference to the fertility of Lacan's use of the concept of castration and the unravelling of his veiled notion of masquerade. But for the moment let us focus on the idea of being versus having, and on the function of the phallus as enabling us to 'pinpoint the structures which will govern the relations between the sexes'. On the face of it, the phallus is being referred to here as something the male has and the female has not, something which belongs to the gent and is enacted and/or wished for by the lady. But it is obvious that the situation is not so simple, if only because of the impact of the Imaginary dimension – let alone the empirical question of what women might actually want (as in Cixous' comment, quoted in Chapter 2, 'I don't want a penis . . .'). The complication for men is that we might think we own something but can never be sure, because so much of that thing is a fantasy concerning potency – we never know if it is, or we are, good enough. This uncertainty and sense of distance from the ideal can then lead us into an obsessive and impossible search for the truly desirable, potent phallus to replace the one we have.

In this connection, here is the rather troubled, self-conscious comment of a man:

> Belonging is a male problem in our existing system of man and woman, 'masculinity' and 'femininity'; it is the obsession of my identity as a man, getting things straight, knowing where I am and what I have and where she is and what she hasn't.
>
> (Heath, 1987, p. 16)

'Having' the phallus attached to oneself is no guarantee of stability of identity; quite the contrary, it forces the man into an obsession with 'getting things straight' and a terror of loss which must seem comic to the penis-free woman. So much is made of it that the phallus becomes a burden to the man; living up to it becomes the necessary condition of masculinity, which is therefore always in danger of being betrayed and undermined. What is it to 'have an identity as a man'? It is, according to this view, to have everything straight and in its (intended) place.

The difficulty of sustaining a masculine identity produces and is constructed by a number of effects. Much of the excess of masculine sexuality seems to derive from the desperate struggle to retain a conviction of phallic mastery – of potency – when what is being experienced is the impossibility of measuring up to the fantasy of the full phallus (see Chapter 5 for a fuller discussion). 'The clenched fist, the bulging muscles, the hardened jaws, the proliferation of phallic symbols – they are all straining after what can hardly ever be achieved, the embodiment of the phallic mystique' (Dyer, 1982, p. 72; quoted in Segal, 1990, p. 89). Even in softer circles, amongst men who struggle to find themselves a place in feminism, there is a tendency to accept (or 'admire', in Heath's [1987] terminology) the force and otherness of the feminist project, only to take it over and make it into another arena for masculine competitiveness. Quoting and criticising a statement of Terry Eagleton's about the insufficiency of feminist theory, Heath (1987, p. 12) writes, 'None of this is written to be cleverer than or superior to Terry Eagleton . . . , even if in the reflection of writing I cannot – do not know how to – avoid the male image, the image of bettering, of asserting superiority.' In the same collection, Smith writes:

> men can, – perhaps, or at least – help the effort to forestall the academic institutionalisation of feminism. They may be able to take an interrogative, but sympathetic role. Indeed, from the point of their impossible – provocative, offensive, troublesome – position in or near feminism, they might be able to help keep in view the referent which most of our current theory is all too eager to defer.
>
> (Smith, 1987, p. 39)

It is not difficult to see the colonising impulse at work here again, as men find their position of mastery threatened and undermined, particularly by a system (or plurality of systems) of thought that excludes men, or can at least make do without them. The all-female world is a terrible threat, apparently offering no place within it for the third party, the man (no 'Name of the Father' here, it seems). What better strategy than to offer to take the position of difference, to protect feminism from the dangers of 'institutionalisation' – empty narcissism – to show how much a man is needed, what umbrella he can hold up in the rain? Are these masters of the feminine any different from the flexors of muscles, all running to find a way to shore up the phallus as it becomes clearer and clearer that, in itself, there is nothing predetermined and natural about it at all? (An infinite regress can creep in here too, as I write this critique of masculine strategies of power into my own masculine book on gender. Men 'find *their* position of mastery threatened', is what appears a few sentences above. But we have to go on somehow, creating hostages to fortune all the time.)

Lacan is a master of ambiguity here. On the one hand, the phallus is the primary signifier, producing difference and forcing men and women apart. The Symbolic order only comes into operation when the father speaks; woman is excluded from the system, though she (in Imaginary guise) has a crucial role in defining its boundaries – without the woman, everything would be the same, so no specific masculinity could exist. Fascinated by castration, Lacan pretends that the phallus is not a masculine symbol; but this may be just another phallic move, veiling the particular nature of the phallus as masculine. Nevertheless, this nature is revealed in the effects of the phallus, which are to make the symbols of the male the determinants of the Symbolic order as a whole. So the phallus does actually represent male mastery, despite Lacan's apparent denials. Yet, the phallus is also something lost and/or losable – it reminds the boy of the threat that what he most prizes will be taken away; hence, it is a constant source of anxiety about power.

In addition to this, there is something still more fragile in the fantasy of masculine autonomy and control.

> Lacan points to the exceptional anxiety involved in taking on a masculine identification. Indeed, the figure of the male *qua* male might be called the cultural lie which maintains that sexual identity can be personified by making difference itself a position.
>
> (Ragland-Sullivan, 1991, p. 51)

Masculinity has the appearance of being defined by something positive – that which the male has and the female lacks. However, emphasising this, as Freud did and as Lacan appears to do, is a masculine strategy employed to deny the implications of the converse, that masculinity is defined negatively, as that which is not feminine. There are two senses in which this is the case. The concrete psychological one is the way in which the Oedipus complex operates as a division between child and mother: the boy only becomes a boy through renunciation of the feminine, not just as object of desire but also as subject of identification, and incorporation into the very general, very 'other' paternal Law. More abstractly, Lacan consistently employs a structural linguistic heuristic for psychoanalysis that defines presence only in relation to difference – only in relation to that which is not also there. Laplanche and Leclaire (1966, p. 154) explain, 'there is no signifier that does not refer to the absence of others and that is not defined by its place in the system'. Lacan tries to exempt the phallus from this stricture, but not wholeheartedly: the phallus can only be seen as whole and positive in content when it is in the register of the Imaginary; that is, this wholeness is a fantasy. So the Symbolic order, the primacy of the phallic signifier and the content of masculinity are given as a series of oppositions, as established only by comparison with what they are not. And amongst these assertions and counter-assertions about the nature of masculinity, there is even some doubt about whether the phallus is symbolised by the penis or whether something more feminine can take its place, as in the quotation from Ragland-Sullivan given earlier or as in Grosz's (1990, p. 119) comment that the penis 'does not have the sole right of alignment with the phallus' but can be substituted for by objects such as 'the whole of a woman's body'. Are men necessary? Living in doubt is never an easy situation.

The ambiguity of the phallus is something integral to its function: it operates both to divide the sexes and to encourage a fantasy of oneness. Grosz puts her finger on it, metaphorically at least, in the following quotation which emphasises the way the phallus can only function in an economy of intersubjectivity, in which the 'owner' of the phallus is dependent on the recognition and desire of the other who apparently does not have it. The master depends on the slave, making the slave the master.

> As the logical or grammatical copula, [the phallus] serves to connect two terms together while disappearing or evacuating itself of any identity of its own. It functions to unite (and disappear) or to separate and divide. This fundamental ambiguity or duplicity in the term will provide a vulnerable, contradictory point within male relations and sexual domination. As signifier, the phallus is not an object to be acquired or an identity to be achieved. It is only through the desire of the other that one's own position – as either being or having the phallus – is possible.
>
> (Grosz, 1990, p. 125)

As ever, Lacan is more elusive than this: the idea of the phallus as 'copula' is included in his 'One might say' list of those reasons why the phallus is primary signifier, which he dispatches by saying that they are 'veils'. Lacan presents his phallus, and himself, as self-sufficient. Nevertheless, to develop past the phallic phase one needs to form relationships; this means that some kind of intersubjectivity must exist, and that 'I' and 'thou' have to be clearly differentiated and seen in relation to each other. Phallic mastery itself needs recognition and desire from the other; take that away and both phallus and man, perhaps even Lacan, dissolve into dust.

The idea of the woman as the other in the phallic economy of the Symbolic order has constantly crept into these notes. It is a masculine 'Other' that initiates the Symbolic: the Name of the Father places a barrier between the boy and his mother, between the self and the object of desire. But it seems to be the fantasy of the woman as something outside the Symbolic which is required to keep the Symbolic order in place, to set its boundaries, its inclusions and exclusions. Something ambiguous operates here too, something to do with desire and with femininity – something that again calls into question the masculine world. Ragland-Sullivan (1991, p. 62) writes, 'The definition of the masculine (not man *per se*) is that which believes itself to be whole. But beware the paradox: whole in relation to what *he is not* – woman. That is, man is a failed woman.' In this reading, the organisation of femininity is different from that of masculinity: the latter is premised on difference, on being superior to, other than, the one who is lacking; femininity, on the other hand, is built around sameness: the woman has 'identified with similarity as an identity position' (*ibid.*).

The possibility of such an asymmetrical situation needs to be questioned. If one side is defined by difference, can the other be absorbed in an economy of the same? This argument is akin to that of object relations theory, in which the pre-Oedipal position of the girl is taken to be one of identity with the mother, a position that produces her gender characteristics with all their struggles concerning autonomy and potency. The boy, by contrast, is constructed out of difference, out of the mother's own definition of him as 'not-I'. It is this that produces the male's unrelieved search for something which is 'same', his precarious gender identity based on differentiation from others, and his characteristic incapacity and terror when faced with demands for intimacy and mutually dependent relationships. As will be argued in Chapter 5, this account has some important insights to offer when considering the trajectories of masculine and feminine development, particularly in relation to mothering and to men's fear of women. But it also reads like the imaginary picture which Lacan has identified as a fantasy of the Other: that somewhere there is something whole, which needs no other, which knows itself as itself and is complete. Ragland-Sullivan writes that the woman 'knows no-one is whole because she has not identified with difference as an imaginary universal, an identity fiction of autonomy' (*ibid.*); but in this knowledge of non-wholeness she becomes complete, she has seen and absorbed the truth. The woman becomes idealised as phallus, again.

There is a great deal in 'The Meaning of the Phallus' which is concerned with the tensions of 'having' and 'being' the phallus, mixed in with desire and with sexual difference. Lacan devotes some space to his famous distinction between need, demand and desire – between what is required by the human subject, what becomes translated into communicable symbols, and what is left over, as an unfillable ache or gap between the hope and its realisation. As needs are put into signifying form – as they become or 'are subject to' demand – so they become alienated; that is, they become converted into a message in which what is being demanded is not some specific satisfaction, but complete affirmation or recognition. 'Demand', states Lacan (p. 80), 'in itself bears on something other than the satisfactions which it calls for. It is a demand for a presence or an absence'. The fantasy is that the other can completely give itself up to the subject; but the actual impossibility of this means that demand is left unfulfilled, reflecting back on the subject as lack of recognition, as something still to be desired.

> Hence it is that demand cancels out the particularity of anything which might be granted by transmuting it into a proof of love, and the very satisfactions of need which it obtains are degraded as being no more than a crushing of the demand for love.
>
> (Lacan, pp. 80–1)

It is in this gap between need and demand, between what can be fulfilled and what is impossible, that desire arises. In a famous if unusually reductionist (thus probably veiled) proposition, Lacan takes this as an opportunity to dictate the nature of desire:

> Thus desire is neither the appetite for satisfaction, nor the demand for love, but the difference resulting from the subtraction of the first from the second, the very phenomenon of their splitting.
>
> (Lacan, p. 81)

As complete love is impossible, as each subject is split by the operations of language and the unconscious, so every human subject finds her or himself looking for proofs of love, and standing in as the cause of the other's desire. Here is the 'formula' Lacan places at the heart of sexual life: 'that for each partner in the relation, the subject and the Other, it is not enough to be the subjects of need, nor objects of love, but they must stand as the cause of desire' (*ibid.*).

'They must stand as the cause of desire.' Each subject strives to find the worm of desire in the other and to become it – to arouse in the other recognition of the necessity of the subject's existence. The mother's desire is for the phallus, so the child strives to become the phallus. Indeed, it is the discovery that the *mother* does not have the phallus that is taken by Lacan as decisive for the castration complex, for it both offers a way for the child to be the cause of the mother's desire, and signifies the power of the threat of castration (or for the girl, the nostalgia for what once was). For every subject, male and female, desire is a constant reminder of incompleteness: it is always the desire of the Other which has to be recognised 'meaning, the Other as itself a subject divided by the signifying *Spaltung*' (Lacan, p. 83), that is, as something split.

Becoming the cause of the other's desire creates a specific place for the woman in – or rather, outside – the masculine sexual-symbolic order. Being phallic in origin, this order is defined around the having versus not-having economy of the male, an economy different from that fantasised as characteristic of the female. Heath takes up the Lacanian slogan 'there is no sexual relation' to provide the following eloquent explanation of the function of the exclusion of the woman:

Relation, the idea of relation, depends on an imaginary other who will complement me as one, make up for the fact of division, stop the loss of identity. Women have been powerfully represented and held as 'woman' to be this other and then, the pressure of the reality of women, feared and hated and attacked as the imaginary other of 'woman' fails and his identity is questioned – at which point she finds herself carried over into the realm of the Other, projected as an enigmatic radical alienness, the back of beyond, and then made up all over again, with talk of her mystery, her ineffable *jouissance*, her closeness to the position of God, and so on.

(Heath, 1987, p. 21)

Heath's account here is both descriptive and explanatory, presenting Lacan's idea and employing it to make sense of the derogation of femininity, the hatred of womanhood and of specific women, which is characteristic of much male fantasy and which can also at times be seen at work in Lacan's own misogynistic musings. The split in masculinity is enforced by the prohibition encapsulated in the Name of the Father; this creates a sensation of otherness – of the Other – which exists as a fantasised place of 'true speech', of the (masculine) Law, but also of (feminine) wholeness and completion. Together with narcissistic fantasies of return, this process feeds the masculine fantasy that somewhere there is a fulfilment which it is possible to achieve; given that his existence as male is structured around difference, then it is the other in the form of the not-male that comes to serve as the ideal of this Other. In this sense, the woman becomes the phallus for the man – that which holds all the answers, which stands outside the system of the Symbolic, which when encountered will make him complete.

THE WOMAN FOR THE MAN

The subject is split, claims Lacan, irreparably so; the fantasy of wholeness, for instance of complete integration of the different elements of the personality, is precisely a fantasy, an element in the Imaginary order which is undermined by the Symbolic. Whatever claims concerning the possibility of integration might be asserted by other schools of psychoanalysis, Lacan knows them to be false; the condition of human subjecthood is to be subject to the law which says, there is no One (no Other of the Other). But this does not prevent us searching for it: in religion, in psychoanalysis, in grand theory; in the relationship to God, in the words of the analyst, in fetishism of the cultural guru, even in Lacan. For men, one systematic element in this is the construction of a representation of the Other as woman, an idealised image drawing upon nostalgia for early infancy, but also precisely an idealisation, an image made whole and good by virtue of splitting off and repressing its negative characteristics. Such idealisations are easily punctured: Lacan (1972–3, p. 144) states, 'There is no such thing as *The* Woman, where the definite article stands for the universal. There is no such thing as *The* Woman since of her essence . . . she is not all'. So when the woman does not deliver the goods, when the reality of women is found to be different from the fantasy of 'The Woman', this negativity floods back in. The terror of femininity returns, alongside the uncertainty produced by the masculine need for the feminine and by men's consciousness of the precariousness of gender identity in the face of feminine recalcitrance – women's unwillingness to be forced into a position in which they enact men's fantasies. At its extreme, this makes for violence, for a howl of rage from the man with no Other, with nothing to fill the vacancy that inhabits his desire.

The woman, as an image and a wish, is excluded from the masculine order but operates as its anchor, both as ideal and as a concentrated point of darkness. The rapid fluctuation from one to the other of these elements is a cliché of critical analysis: from madonna to whore, often with no boundary in between. Masculinity needs femininity, needs the feminine ideal, but dreads it and hates the impossibility of its attainment. Lacan (p. 84) comments that even when the man 'manages to satisfy his demand for love in his relationship to the woman', he will feel dissatisfaction and look elsewhere: 'his own desire for the phallus will throw up its signifier in the form of a persistent divergence towards "another woman" who can signify this phallus under various guises, whether as virgin or as prostitute'. There is no end to it, no romance or happy ever after, only the illusion and trickery of Imaginary love.

Not only is this point of view pessimistic, but it is unequivocally male: the only articulation of the position of the woman is in relation to the order and experience of masculinity. Indeed, it has been commented upon by several authors that Lacan re-enacts the dynamic his theory describes. He denigrates women ceaselessly, for instance as 'not knowing what they are saying' (1972–3, p. 144 – see Chapter 6), or for their supposed silence on feminine sexuality; he plays seductively to them as if their desire would, and should, be only for him. But he also fantasises something specific in femininity which leaves the masculine behind, something ineffable and whole, a complete experience of pleasure which always remains untranslated as '*jouissance*' – at its extreme, a self-sufficiency, a 'jouissance wrapped in its own contiguity' (Lacan, 1964, p. 97). Grosz (1990), in her 'feminist introduction' to Lacan, notes how he 'seems to want to retain some of the allure and the mystery of the Eternal Feminine' (p. 140) but also finds a way of doing this that itself denies women anything to call their own.

Woman experiences a *jouissance beyond the phallus*. But if this enigmatic *jouissance* is attributed to women as the mark of her resistance to the

Other, at the same time this *jouissance* is, by that fact, strictly outside of articulation and is thus *unknowable*. Lacan accords women the possibility of refusing a pleasure and desire that is not theirs, but not of claiming one that *is* theirs.

(Grosz, 1990, p. 139)

To repeat: 'If Lacan begs women to tell him in what their pleasure consists, he is not prepared to hear what they have to say' (Grosz, 1990, p. 146). If one is to take seriously something articulated by Gallop (1988, p. 125), one of the things women might have to say is that 'it remains an open question whether there truly exists any adult sexuality, whether there is any masculinity that is beyond the phallic phase, that does not need to equate femininity with castration'. This is an accusation levelled at all men, including the one who claims to go beyond the phallic phase, Lacan; he too seems to have little place for women other than as fantasy ideal or whore.

What happens to the feminine in all this? 'The Meaning of the Phallus' focuses on castration; the feminine is presented as the other side of this, as that which is already castrated and therefore cannot be subject of desire – if desire is defined in the masculine register, as Lacan appears to prefer. The woman seeks what she has not, and the way in which she seeks it is given to her by the formula mentioned earlier, that 'for each partner in the relation, the subject and the Other, it is not enough to be the subjects of need, nor objects of love, but they must stand as the cause of desire' (Lacan, p. 81). With desire organised around the phallus, and with masculinity defined in terms of a continuing struggle to 'have' the phallus – to avoid castration – 'standing as the cause of desire' for the woman means representing the phallus to the man. At its simplest, this is the process of becoming the romantic 'Other', the One who will complete the man through the fact of her difference, her fantasised complementarity. In the explicit discussion of the phallus to be found in 'The Meaning of the Phallus', however, Lacan stresses that the woman seeks to 'be' the phallus by taking on the appearance of wholeness, of the final object of desire. As such, the woman strives to be something which in fact only *seems* to be real, and the dynamic of sexual difference becomes entwined with 'masquerade' and a descent into comedy.

This follows from the intervention of an 'appearing' which gets substituted for the 'having' so as to protect it on one side and to mask its lack on the other, with the effect that the ideal or typical manifestations of behaviour in both sexes, up to and including the act of sexual copulation, are entirely propelled into comedy.

(Lacan, p. 84)

At one level, the woman acts in masquerade in the straightforward and well-documented sense that 'femininity' is a representation constructed primarily through masculine discourse, as the object of male fantasy to which individual women are asked to succumb: 'It is for what she is not that she expects to be desired as well as loved' (*ibid.*). Resisting this alienated construction of femininity has been a struggle long engaged in by feminists as they attempt to create a representation or set of representations of womanhood other than that given by patriarchy, including evolving modes of display that are self-consciously chosen and are not reducible to masquerade.

Lacanian ambiguity, however, puts more into this. The woman acts in masquerade in the deeper sense that, although her existence is constructed as 'other' to the phallic order of the Symbolic, she must nevertheless speak from a position within that order if she is to have a voice in language and culture at all. Hence, 'when she speaks as an "I" it is never clear that she speaks (of or as) herself. She speaks in a mode of masquerade, an imitation of the masculine phallic subject' (Grosz, 1990, p. 72). Moreover, 'The woman can be the phallus only through semblance, masquerade, or appearance, but this ensures she is also *not* the phallus. Paradoxically, to be affirmed as the phallus is to be annihilated as woman' (Grosz, 1990, p. 132). The woman's place is given in a male order; taking up the position alienates her from any possibility of being subject of her own desire, yet it is also the only way in which she can exist. Something else happens here too, on the other side of Lacan's depreciation of women. Once again his text re-enacts the dynamic: the woman has no voice, does not exist; yet she embodies the subversion of the order that so marginalises her. Adopting a very conventional and undeconstructed approach to gender, Lacan argues that, whereas libido is masculine, all display is feminine, even 'virile display'. The woman is presented as surface, as play, as misleading object of desire. The female body is taken as that which can fulfil desire, but it is all masquerade; even if the man feels for a while satisfied, 'his own desire for the phallus will throw up its signifier in the form of a persistent divergence towards "another woman" ' (Lacan, p. 84) – there is no end to this seeking. There are at least two ways of looking at this. The first asserts that the woman's appearance is a sham; she is fraudulent. On the other hand, this sham status actually expresses a truth: that there is no 'One', no complete Other which can offer the fulfilment of desire. Femininity thus embodies the Lacanian propositions that desire is constituted precisely by lack and gap, and that to fail to accept this as the condition of human subjectivity is to live in illusion. In this sense, the woman stands as some kind of truth rooted in subversion of the masculine fantasy that complete stability and ownership of the other is possible.

Ragland-Sullivan offers the following thought on the subversion of masculinity by masquerade.

Because the 'gift' of lack robs us of certainty and takes a bite out of ego and body – the masculine and feminine delineating different positions taken in regard to lack – the feminine masquerade automatically poses a question, while masculine identification with law, logos or authority tries to stop the question. Yet, paradoxically, *his* effort at mastery shows a lack – a lie as the basis of the symbolic – while *her* lack of position is unbearable in the real.

(Ragland-Sullivan, 1991, pp. 75–6)

In this reading, masculinity closes things up, tries to deny castration, to hang on to the possession of the penis as a symbolic equivalent to possession of the phallus. It is the masculine that is engaged in masquerade here – a pretence that domination arises naturally from anatomy, that there is a biological inscription of patriarchy making resistance useless. The masculine seeks confirmation, seeks to shore up boundaries; as has been shown many times (e.g. Theweleit, 1977) there is a close connection between this attribute of masculinity and authoritarian, fascist and racist modes of political action and organisation. Femininity, through its play of surfaces, its multifarious-ness and its elusiveness, can be seen as the enemy of such confirmation; it always speaks of difference, of the impossibility of being pinned down.

This picture of masculinity suggests that it exists only by keeping the other at bay, by avoiding castration; but it also exists only in relation to the Other as desired object, as that which might confirm the male by acknowledging his ownership of the phallus. Femininity, by virtue of its otherness in the Symbolic order, its position as 'already castrated', is both the desired other and a reminder of the possibility of dissolution of gender itself. In masquerade, the woman can come to represent the phallus with her whole body; but she also reveals that this process is only one of mask and display. Yet, this is also the phallic point: once again, it is worth recalling that Lacan says that 'the phallus can only play its role as veiled' (Lacan, p. 82); veils and the phallus are inextricably linked. In her masquerade, the woman not only acts as other to the Symbolic order, thus defining its boundaries; she also shows that 'the phallus' is itself a process of search and play, of enigma and thus of desire; and notwithstanding its appropriation by masculine discourse, it 'belongs' to no-one at all.

In the end, this seems to have brought us back to a traditional image of femininity as that which subverts the established order, as the power of a 'nature' which is always slippery and unreliable. To some extent, this simply repeats the masculine fantasy of female otherness, as something to be repudiated because of the way it upsets order and rationality ('science'), but also as something secretly longed for because of its passion and excitement ('nature'). The Lacanian algebra of phallus and Symbolic rework this traditional image, incorporating it into a discourse on language and the unconscious that reveals the existence of something both precious and impossible – the fantasy positions of masculine and feminine constantly disrupted by desire. Femininity, most explicitly through the concepts of masquerade and *jouissance*, undermines the claims of masculinity to mastery: there is no complete master, as the phallus is not something one can ever wholly own. But this does not necessarily put an end to illusion, or to the pursuit of domination, as the next chapter will discuss.

Moreover, there is an element here which has not yet been properly explored. Towards the end of 'The Meaning of the Phallus', Lacan makes a reference to the mother.

> Clinical practice demonstrates that the test of the desire of the Other is not decisive in the sense that the subject learns from it whether or not he has a real phallus, but inasmuch as he learns that the mother does not. This is the moment of experience without which no symptomatic or structural consequence (that is, phobia or *penisneid*) referring to the castration complex can take effect.
>
> (Lacan, p. 83)

At its simplest, this is a conventional Freudian statement that the male subject's awareness of the existence of female genital 'insufficiency' is necessary for castration anxiety to have its effect and therefore for the Oedipus complex to be resolved, so setting into motion the patterns of identification and repression which Lacan characterises as the Symbolic order. But the explicit reference here to the *mother's* lack of phallus is a reminder of the extent to which masculinity – the status of supposedly not being castrated – is built upon the shaky foundations of distance from the mother, of being other than the mother of whom one once was part. The Oedipus complex is the structure within which the father's word is heard, denying access to the mother's body as a source of sexual gratification; but something more powerful even than that prohibition is also at work. Looking at the female 'lack', the male perceives an apparent failure to specify a limit and location for sexuality, and consequently feels a terror of dissolution, of falling back and in, of losing his precariously attained identity. It is not just *domination* which is placed in jeopardy here, but masculine *existence*. This underpins at least some of the male's idealisation and terror of femininity, experienced as that which is most desired and most feared, that which at one and the same time gives and takes away. The masculine response to this, within a symbolic order constructed around difference and exclusion, is to make the woman into a goddess and then do everything possible to keep her in chains. Thus, in the midst of approbation there is misogyny; where there is adoration there is sexual violence. Phallic uncertainty and the power of the mother: in these are the seeds of masculine sexuality sown.

NOTE

1. References to Lacan's work in this chapter are, unless otherwise specified, to 'The Meaning of the Phallus', translated by J. Rose in Mitchell and Rose (1982).

Chapter 5

The seeds of masculine sexuality

DECONSTRUCTING MASCULINITY

The previous chapter ended with a statement of the problematic status and origins of masculinity, which seems to be constructed primarily in relation to *difference*, as something which is 'not not-masculine' rather than as something possessing an essence and substance of its own. In this regard, masculinity as a category of experience has more in common with femininity than is often acknowledged. Femininity has, historically and psychoanalytically, usually been defined as the negative of the masculine, as something existing as 'other' and as less worthy, reliable or complete. This means that it has in many respects been an 'empty' category in the sense that it is defined principally in terms of its distance from masculinity rather than in terms of its own positive attributes. Where content is given to the feminine, it is mostly to characterise it either as inferior or as dangerous – for instance, as expressing weakness, passivity, seductiveness and unreliability. In this way, femininity has been constructed to offer a space which can be filled by projected male fantasies, becoming a receptacle for what is disowned and feared.

The fantasy of the woman as castrated yet also castrating is an example of this process, as Theweleit (1977) shows in his account of fascist consciousness. Searching for a way to overcome his anxieties, the man projects them into the woman, who is not credited with any substance of her own; once this is done, he can dominate those anxieties by dominating and excluding her. Sexual difference thus serves the ends of maintaining masculine identity: 'woman', being nothing at all, can be made into anything the man needs her to be. In general, for reasons to be explored in this chapter, this has meant that 'woman' is a space filled by denigration; but sometimes, as part of the same movement of projection, it means engaging in an equally imaginary idealisation.

The struggle against emptiness and towards articulation of a positive content for femininity has always been a major element in the project of feminism (e.g. Segal, 1987). It is also visible in the refutations of the notion of 'penis envy' and related portrayals of femininity as lack which have recurred throughout the history of psychoanalysis (e.g. Mitchell, 1974). As will be discussed in Chapter 6, some contemporary feminist psychoanalysts, particularly those who can be loosely designated as 'post-Lacanian', have been rather successful in this struggle, even if their formulations of feminine presence have never been regarded as unequivocally acceptable, either by feminists (e.g. Mitchell and Rose, 1982) or by sympathetic men (e.g. Elliott, 1992). As a result of such efforts, men and women are now faced with a much stronger assertion of feminine positivity and a more extensive range of concrete representations of feminine capability and power than has perhaps ever previously been the case; and one effect of this is to raise questions about what equivalent alterations might be possible and necessary in the masculine world view.

What might be called the 'reconstruction' of femininity creates problems for masculinity in various ways. An assumption made within the Freudian and Lacanian traditions of psychoanalysis, but equally strongly in much social and feminist criticism from outside the psychoanalytic movement, is that masculinity defines the way in which the world is organised materially and perceived psychologically, and hence that dominant representations of events and experiences are forged from a masculine perspective. Seidler (1989), for example, proposes that at least since Kant and the Reformation, rationality has been the dominant western mode available for construing experience, and rationality and masculinity have been conflated so that each connotes the other. Given the way rationality is conventionally employed to demarcate the boundaries of mental health (Banton *et al.*, 1985), this is an important claim with implications for the marginalisation of femininity and the valorisation of a normative framework for action. It also relates to the way gender insinuates itself into the central polarities around which society is organised: it is *reason* that is taken as marking out what is true and what is false, and reason is seen as something embedded in masculinity but not in femininity. Where reason breaks down, madness ensues; femininity and madness are consequently aligned.

What the reconstruction of femininity does to this set of associations is complex and will be returned to at other points in this chapter. But first and foremost it makes masculine identity itself, especially in relation to its identification with reason, more uncertain and unstable. 'Masculinity' may be a constructed category, but it is one which has been taken to have content, a content premised on the superiority of reason and marked out by comparison with the 'contentless other' category of the feminine. As that latter category is expanded and regenerated, making claims for the presence of a positive feminine consciousness and also contesting the claims of reason to be taken as the 'master system' for comprehending and coding experience, so the assumptions on which conventional modes of masculinity are based become less tenable. Looking inwards, consciously or not, male experience becomes decentred; that is, the adoption of a core masculine identity becomes something that has to be struggled for (much like feminine identity) and cannot just be assumed. When this perspective is adopted, it becomes apparent that the category 'masculine' is not as obvious and as full of content as might have been thought; indeed, it begins to seem that the motivation for all this interest in femininity and its problems might be, in part, to divert attention away from the difficulties of masculinity itself. Freud, for instance, wrote explicitly on femininity and female sexuality, but not on male sexuality as a separate entity; perhaps as a consequence, his work is infused both with gender assumptions made from the perspective of the man and with an ambiguity which the Freudian term 'bisexuality' only partially captures (see Chapter 3). It is not just, therefore, that femininity is a category full of masculine projections (so that exploration of 'femininity' tells us as much about men as about women); it is also that the activity of men in marking out, describing and exploring the feminine 'dark continent' can be understood as an attempt to deal with the anxiety produced by the unstable state of masculine identity. The fact that all this uncertainty is a fairly accurate reflection of the actual standing of gender categories as social constructs does not necessarily make it easier to live with.

To a considerable extent, the problematising of masculinity, which is itself linked to the new questions asked about femininity by feminists, is part of a general dislocation of identity and selfhood in contemporary society (Frosh, 1991). Whereas it might plausibly be claimed that the context in which conventional notions of masculinity arose was characterised by a reasonable stability of ideology and perception, this has not been the case for a considerable time, and more recently (in so-called 'postmodern' culture) the speed of change and degree of instability have become more and more unmanageable, especially for individuals who are caught up in it but exercise no control. Under these circumstances, the masculine order defined by an unbending rational stance cannot sustain itself. 'To be modern', writes Berman (1982, p. 15), 'is to find ourselves in an environment that promises us adventure, power, joy, growth, transformation of ourselves and the world – and, at the same time, that threatens to destroy everything we have, everything we know, everything we are.' There is too much fluctuation and contradiction; as part of this, those who once were dubbed minorities and whose voices were subjugated beneath the dominant discourse of the rational are struggling actively to find some space in which to speak. In this respect, the voices of feminists articulating the significance of emotion and subjectivity have been amongst the most important of those which were previously subjugated and are now newly, if incompletely, freed. And because what these voices say always concerns gender, masculinity has been a prime victim of the disturbing fragmentation of the social and cultural environment. Rationality and reason now look like poor bets to save us on their own, although the contrary tendency to abandon them altogether is another dangerous dead end. Indeed, the whole arena of the 'Imaginary' has become more significant, as people are forced to seek out new ways of representing themselves and their identities (Elliott, 1992) and to recognise the way identity is learned and not given. But widening the sphere of experience and perception to include emotion and acknowledgement of desire – of the unconscious – requires a comprehensive revision of what it means to be a man.

The argument here is that the received tradition identifying masculinity with rationality is giving way in the face of feminist and other cultural critiques, to make the entity 'masculinity' problematic just as it makes problematic the experience of each individual man. As this process continues and escalates, there is an increasing uncertainty about masculine identity, which can be seen both in the direct attempts of some men to be different and in the aggressive reactions of others. As an example of the former process, Seidler (1991) and Segal (1990) are amongst many men and women who stress the necessity of recognising the *heterogeneity* of masculinity. This claim hits at a core feature of masculine ideology: the assumption of universality, of sameness, of the reality of phallic authority. '[It] is crucial', writes Seidler, ' ... to explore the emergence and experiences of different masculinities' (1991, p. 142). Recognition of 'different masculinities' means, for instance, acknowledgement of the specificity of experiences of men who are black or white, homosexual, bisexual or heterosexual, Jewish or Gentile – powerless or powerful. Already, this is a deconstruction: the apparently monolithic nature of masculinity begins to fragment as soon as one investigates it; multiplicity enters in, differences abound; just like women, men are not all the same.

The aggressive strain within masculinity, however, has a longer and more robust history. Segal links it with the deconstruction of masculine identity in the following passage:

> Masculinity is never the undivided, seamless construction it becomes in its symbolic manifestation. The promise of phallic power is precisely this guarantee of total inner coherence, of an unbroken and unbreakable, unquestioned and unquestionable masculinity. Deprived of it, how can men be assured of 'natural' dominance? The antagonisms of gender coalesce with the strains of affirming and maintaining sexual polarities.
>
> (Segal, 1990, p. 102)

As masculinity is experienced as more and more unsustainable in its traditional forms, so, in the absence of other, fuller sources of identity, it is clung to more desperately. The repudiation of homosexuality by heterosexual men is part of this process, as Segal points out: homosexuality is troublingly fantasised as a disruption and 'feminisation' of masculinity and hence must be staved off as part of the defence of the male order itself. Rutherford notes:

> The collective logic of white heterosexual masculine identities is to project our sexual contradictions and repression onto others. Women, gay men and black men are constructed as a threat to the stability of our subjectivity, the potential subverters of our masculine order.
>
> (Rutherford, 1988, p. 66)

Holding on to the ideology of an integrated and rational masculinity, in the face of the deconstruction of masculinity as a whole, can lead to a repudiation of alternatives and hence to a yet more desperate search for identity, experienced as something that has less and less hold on anything stable and secure. And right at the heart of this, as the reference to homosexuality suggests, lie questions about the nature of masculine sexuality.

SEXUALITY AND SUBJECTIVITY

Critical analysis of masculine sexuality, which is no longer taken as 'natural' or completely explained by reference to a putative male biological drive, is part of the larger fragmenting or 'deconstructive' process described above. Nothing can be taken for granted: masculine sexuality is neither something rational and perfectly controlled, nor something which can be reduced to an inner urge requiring occasional or frequent ventilation. Rather, as contemporary criticism takes up the issues sur- rounding the formation and nature of human subjectivity, so it becomes increasingly obvious that sexuality is something integral to the state of the subject; that is, that a full account of sexuality has to be couched in terms of inner, psychological events and not simply in terms of behaviour (e.g. Hollway, 1989).

In this respect, the versions of sexuality described in some sex therapy work, focusing on sexual behaviour without consideration of its subjective underpinnings, preserves a 'masculinist' perspective in which sex is seen as an achievement or set of techniques, rather than as something integral to inner experience and self-definition. The extraordinary strength of homophobic attitudes and practices is one strand of evidence that such a view of sexuality is too limited: identifying and feeling at ease with men's 'own' sexuality seems to be something both necessary and hard to manage, at times producing violent repudiation of anything too threateningly 'other'. Examining masculine sexuality only from the outside can thus be interpreted as an attempt at reassurance based on distancing ourselves from the sexuality of those we study: male sexuality looks like this, this is what men do – and ugly sometimes it seems, when sexual violence is the focus – but it is manageable, adjustable by specific techniques. Such approaches neither aspire to, nor achieve, a serious critique of masculinity itself. Indeed, this instrumental, 'objective' and distanced mode of understanding is an exemplar of the more general masculine identification with reason on which the ideology of gender differentiation has been based. 'The polarity of subject and object', writes Benjamin (1988, p. 216), 'is the enduring skeletal frame of domination'; denying sexuality its place as central to subjectivity is an aspect of this process. The most considerable and troubling questions are not just about what men do, but also about what masculine sexuality 'means', what is at its core, what it feels like to have this possession, this masculine sexual being.

Masculine sexuality and masculinity: these belong together; the former cannot be talked about as distinct from the latter, as a set of behaviours having no bearing on emotion. There is an interior point of view to be uncovered here, a way of exploring masculine sexuality from the perspective of the development of masculine subjectivity: the doing only makes sense in the context of the being. In this context, psychoanalysis becomes a crucial instrument of investigation, for in its various versions it offers the most developed and challenging set of ideas currently available on what might comprise such an 'interior point of view'. Some of these ideas will be presented in this chapter, with particular reference to an issue that has to a considerable extent defined the focus of recent work on masculine sexuality, that of sexual abuse, particularly abuse of children. The next section of this chapter, therefore, looks at the impact of increased awareness of sexual abusiveness for theories of masculinity. Following this, there is an account of one set of psychoanalytic perspectives on masculine development, a set informed particularly by feminist consciousness. Finally, I return to the issue of sexual abuse and try to apply to it some of the insights gleaned from this work, arguing that a full understanding of abusiveness can only be built on the basis of a general theory of masculinity.

ON DOMINANT ABUSE

One source of the contemporary dissatisfaction with traditional masculinity is the specific awareness that the domination so long associated with masculinity is linked with violence and abusiveness. This is, of course, not a new awareness, at least certainly not for women; but feminism has brought with it a much firmer and louder assertion of the links, as well as institutionalised forms of support for women (through, for example, rape crisis centres and women's refuges) than has ever previously been the case. For children, too, specifically in the area of child sexual abuse, there has in recent years been far more recognition of the extent to which victimisation by men is a common experience and of how abused children have been silenced in the past both by their abusers and by the professional and social system (e.g. Glaser and Frosh, 1993). There are, of course, women who abuse children (just as there are lesbian women who are violent towards their lovers – Segal, 1990), but they are a small minority of abusers, despite women, through their caretaking roles, generally having more opportunities (Haugaard and Reppucci, 1988). It is men who predominate in the statistics of sexual abusiveness, and it is consequently in the context of masculinity that the links between sexuality and violence are systematically made.

It is important to acknowledge the impact of the domination/ abusiveness/sexuality network in relation to attitudes towards masculinity. For women, the public recognition of the violence associated with masculine sexuality has legitimised anger and a drive towards separateness, at times amounting to a closing of female ranks around mutual support and a repudiation of all things male. This radical feminist critique, in which masculinity is located as *by nature* oppressive and hence to be either combatted or avoided (through as complete a separation of the sexes as can be managed) is not easy to dismiss. Functionally, it offers solidarity for women and the prospect of effective resistance to men, including resistance to the kind of dependence that stifles the possibilities of escape for women caught in abusive relationships – the main reason, as Segal (1990) and others have shown, why certain women are more vulnerable than others. Such resistance, whatever the response it provokes from men, also makes it less possible to take women for granted; that is, a rhetoric and practice of opposition is now available to challenge any assumption that male domination is preordained as a simple state of nature. Radical feminism asserts that such domination is achieved by force, against the will of a recalcitrant other, who will no longer, if she ever did, take it lying down. Moreover, the content of the critique has been deeply shocking for men, particularly when it has encompassed the claim that women can live without men, that men (in the sense of any particular man) are even unnecessary for procreation. Even for men who are not in their own behaviour abusive or violent, the realisation that some women assume they will be so, and that most women will fear them in some circumstances, has been deeply disturbing, sometimes provoking a misogynistic response (as in Bly's [1990] *Iron John*), but sometimes just producing sadness or despair. Overall, this critical rejection of masculinity makes cracks in the masculine armour that reveal deep and troubling links with destructiveness: 'Do we deserve all this?', 'Is this really how they feel?', 'In every step I take, do I really tread on someone else?'.

With all the force of the radical feminist repudiation of masculinity, however, it does have a mirroring flavour that aligns it with the masculinist ideology it seeks to overcome: rejecting masculinity is too close a parallel to the male rejection of femininity to offer anyone full comfort. In addition, as the following quotation from Seidler (1991) suggests, the rejectionist stance neglects the differentiations currently entering into masculinity, which themselves undermine masculine claims to universal dominance. That is, by lumping all men together into one disavowed group, radical feminism reiterates the 'one and whole' mythology of masculinity – that all men are characterised by the same attributes of univocal command, homogeneous demand, smooth rationality and violent force. Seidler criticises this element of feminism as follows:

> It has been an enduring feature of radical feminist work to place issues of male violence at the centre of an understanding of social relations, although often this has been done in a way that forecloses the possibilities of men to change. In this context it is crucial not to treat masculinity as a unified and homogeneous category, fixed within particular relations of power, but to explore the emergence and experiences of different masculinities.
>
> (Seidler, 1991, p. 142)

The mentality of them-and-us is one which has to be avoided if any reconstruction of sexual relations is to occur; it is apparent not just in fascism, but also more generally in masculine ideology, with its fantasy of a truly rational state of masculine authority defending civilisation against the potential dissolution produced by immersion in the swamp of femininity. Undifferentiating rejectionism misses the opportunity to carve out a space for the worm of doubt to enter into this fantasy, the worm carrying the suggestion that, 'We are not all, every one of us, the same'. Consequently, rejectionism shares in the ideology of wholeness: there is nothing you can do with masculinity except oppose it, it is so monolithic, it will always strive to dominate; some men may seem like allies, but in the end they will stick to their own. An optimistic element in the deconstruction of masculinity is that, just like femininity, masculinity does not necessarily have to be fixed into just one mode of being; there could be space for change, if only conditions will allow it. Feminist rejectionism, by dismissing or belittling the possibility of such change, is in danger of reinforcing the already considerable barriers to it actually taking place.

Of course the self-hating man is just as irritating as the macho, and self-hatred derives from some of the same sources. Seidler suggests that there is an 'ongoing polarity within masculine experience, between self-hatred and idealisation' (1991, p. 91), with the struggle of men to live up to an externally imposed self-image (rational, in control) always being likely to make them despise themselves and what they do. But this is of no use to anyone if it simply produces an apology; what is needed is a surer understanding of what produces male abusiveness so that it can actually be challenged rather than simply denied. This is why critical examination of masculinity in the light of the feminist critique, analysis of what it is that feeds male abusiveness – why the force has to be so much with us – is an important project, one that can move us on, different perhaps, but towards togetherness.

MASCULINITY DISSOLVED

Theories aspiring to articulation of the interior point of view are not necessarily themselves immune from androcentric assumptions. Lacan, for example, as discussed in the previous chapter, identifies the woman as 'Other', deep in the psyche and deeply rejected from the Symbolic web of culture. Lacan, however, is no innovator here. Freud also has a misogynistic way about him, not just in his direct assertions of female inferiority (e.g. 'The fact that women must be regarded as having little sense of justice is no doubt related to the predominance of envy in their mental life' – Freud, 1933, p. 168), but also in the assumptions he makes concerning the underlying gender structures of mental life. 'The little girl is a little man', he writes (1933, p. 152); sexual libido is active, *therefore* it must be construed as masculine. Sexuality is something which, in a way familiar to men and characteristic of male-dominated public as well as private life, can be thought of as *doing*, as acting on the other, pushing and shoving and thrusting and achieving. It is a relatively short step from this idea to that of sex as technique, rather than as a mode of relationship or a state of being. From this perspective, the feminine (defined as passive but also as an enigma, because feminine pleasure does not make sense from the point of view of a masculine economy premised on the notion of desire as activity) is perceived as something 'other': mysterious and, like 'mother' nature itself, a state which is potentially engulfing and threatening, but also a site of great riches, to be explored and conquered. Men need to understand it, to struggle with it, precisely because it is so alien, so much the 'dark continent' threatening to overwhelm us if we do not deal with it first.

As discussed in Chapter 4, Lacanian theory has claimed the phallus as the signifier of the Symbolic order in which gender inequality is embedded. Translated into more concrete depictions of masculinity, this has become an argument that 'possessing' the phallus is impossible, but that men are more able than women to act and experience themselves *as if* they were in possession of it, given its cultural conflation with the male penis. Here is a characteristic account of this kind:

> *If* The phallus is the key signifier of difference ... then masculinity becomes set up as the norm and femininity can only exist as absence, as what masculinity is not. Of course no-one actually possesses the phallus but men are able to make identifications with this symbol in a way that women are not.
>
> (Moore, 1988, p. 172)

By way of contrast, this is Segal's rendering of the same issue:

> Bolstered by the multifaceted reality of men's power, the phallus, as a symbol, is not, however, available for individual men to possess. It is that which they attempt to possess, or perhaps to reject; or maybe that which they approach with uncertainty and disquiet.
>
> (Segal, 1990, p. 210)

Both writers, in the Lacanian tradition, assume the reality of the phallus as prime signifier of difference, but for Moore (much like Mitchell, 1974, in her influential articulation of the value of Freudian theory for understanding the perpetuation of patriarchy) this produces an automatic link between masculinity and power, whereas for Segal it is problematic for men – something they might like, or feel they ought to have, but also something that constantly reminds them of the elusiveness of real power and of their own inadequacy. The important distinction is perhaps that made by Segal, between the 'multifaceted reality of men's power' – that is, the way men are structurally (socially, economically and politically) dominant over women – and the experience of powerlessness characteristic of many individual men and possibly, if Seidler (1991) is correct in his assertions concerning the impact of industrial decline on masculine identity, becoming more significant all the time. Lacanian theory clarifies this by implying that the imaginary status of the phallus as the key signifier of difference sets up an unattainable fantasy of power for men, so that men's actual and irrevocable experience of not being able to 'attain the phallus' leads them to experience themselves as lacking and empty. In this reading, male dominance is built on a desperate denial of inner emptiness; it is a defence against dissolution and the unmasking of the emptiness of the masculine identity. Not that this is necessarily any comfort to the women and children who are the victims of male violence, but at least it begins to explain the rigidity and passion of the masculine response to threat.

As described in Chapter 4, Lacan (1958, p. 82) plays with the idea that there may be something intrinsic to the choice of the phallus as signifier of desire which links it to the masculine sexual organ ('One might say that this signifier is chosen as what stands out as most easily seized upon in the real of sexual copulation . . . One might also say that by virtue of its turgidity, it is the image of the vital flow as it is transmitted in generation'). However, this idea is entertained only in order to dismiss it in favour of an assertion of the invisibility of the phallus itself as more than an emanation of various powerful effects ('All these propositions merely veil over the fact that the phallus can only play its role as veiled'). It is neither one thing nor another; the phallus, which we take as the mark of masculine authority, only 'plays its role as veiled' – it is hidden, not amenable to pinning down, not a reliable defining point for masculine identity. Women may indulge in masquerade (Lacan, 1958, p. 84), thus not having any real essence, but if men claim dominance through the phallus they are in for a sore surprise. The penis, which men do have, is not the phallus, for the phallus is a symbol rather than a substance; all those bemusing male impotences are linked to this. What seems most obvious ('what stands out') is in fact inscrutable ('veiled') and unavailable to possession – the real organ cannot match the imaginary one, and the more one tries to make it do so, the more incorrigible is the failure likely to be.

> Here we have in a nutshell a constituting element of male sexual ideology. A man is only a man in so far as he is capable of using his penis as an instrument of power. It is a weapon by means of which he can subdue a woman. But . . . this belief in the overwhelming drive of male sexuality is undermined by the reality of sexual experience.
>
> (Brittan, 1989, p. 47)

The myth of masculinity is that power is destined by anatomy, and that this power takes its form from the 'oneness' of male sexual display – the upswelling, integrated, wholeness of being. Ranged with this is the emphasis on rationality identified by Seidler (1989) and many others; thinking is made into an aspect of domination, with the centrality of the distinction between subject and object (connoting masculine and feminine) being used as a further boost to masculine defence against loss of control. But behind all this, lurking somewhere in the relatively unarticulated regions of men's sexual and emotional experience, is a hidden recognition of the *incoherence* of the masculine state, of the way its ideological claims to effectiveness and power are built on a continuing denial of weakness and dependence. It is in this sense that Seidler can claim, 'Masculinity is an essentially negative identity learnt through defining itself against emotionality and connectedness' (1989, p. 7). An 'essentially negative identity': this does not suggests something filled with phallic power, but something built around a flight from something else.

HIS-STORY

The conventional view of masculine sexuality, shared by Freud, is that it is active and driven, and that the core of male sexual fantasy is the expression of his (subject) desire through use of the (object) other. As Segal (1990) points out, however, this view is challenged by homosexuality ('gay sexuality offers further confirmation of the ambiguity, even ultimately, the unintelligibility, of the mapping of active/passive onto masculine/feminine' – p. 151), which is probably one of the many sources of homophobia amongst heterosexual men ('The most persistent myths surrounding contemporary conceptions of homosexuality are bound up with men's need for the gender reassurance they obtain from the assertion of heterosexual interests and behaviour' – pp. 134–5). In addition, there is a more general pattern of evidence concerning men's sexuality that reveals the problematic status of this 'phallic' model.

> Whatever the meanings attached to 'the act' of sexual intercourse, for many men it confirms a sense of ineptness and failure: the failure to satisfy women ... for many men it is precisely through sex that they experience their greatest uncertainties, dependence and deference in relation to women ... And certainly for many men it is precisely through experiencing themselves as powerless and submissive that they experience the greatest sexual pleasure.
>
> (Segal, 1990, p. 212)

There are a number of elements in this claim which are of importance when considering the organisation of masculine sexuality. The phallic model suggests that men achieve satisfaction through expression of their sexual drive, and that it is the expression of this drive in the context of power and domination of the other that makes it satisfying. But what the literature suggests is that this male-centred model is at variance with the actual experience of many men, whose sexual encounters with women are organised around a pole of insufficiency and disappointment, and a search for reassurance which does not always meet with success. Grosz (1990, pp. 131–2) asserts, in Lacanian terms, that 'the man can be affirmed as phallic only through the other who desires (and therefore lacks) what he has', but this affirmation is never complete and is often withheld, due to the man's 'failure to satisfy' the woman. Segal's claim that for many men, 'it is precisely through sex that they experience their greatest uncertainties, dependence and deference in relation to women', suggests that women are being perceived as more powerful and complete than men can ever hope to be. Men thus objectify but also idealise women as possessing something they themselves do not have. This directly contradicts the traditional Freudian notion of the woman as the one constituted by lack (penis envy), but is in line with the Lacanian idea that the woman is fantasised as the 'Other' through whom completion might be achieved.

This fantasy of the woman's greater power and the potential inability of the man to satisfy her desire can also be seen in the limited theoretical articulation of what masculine sexuality might consist in (phallic penetration and a search for reassurance that castration has not occurred), compared to the fuller and more evocative – not to say, romantic and unrealistic – attributes claimed to be associated with female sexual pleasure. Heath puts it like this:

> In the overall system of sexuality that is tightened to perfection in the nineteenth century and that still today determines so powerfully in so

many ways the facts of our lives, male sexuality is repetition, female sexuality is query.

(Heath, 1987, p. 13)

The 'query' concerns a decentring of sexuality from the limits of phallic penetrative functionality to a broader, more intense and more fluid appropriation of pleasure. This is termed '*jouissance*' in the fashionable literature on the subject, meaning something like an ineffable and overwhelmingly ecstatic climactic experience. *Jouissance* has come to be seen as an attribute of feminine sexuality – women as 'perpetual motion machines programmed to produce their own rapture' (Bowie, 1991, p. 149). One of the many ironies inherent in Lacanian theory is that this element of feminine pleasure is both downgraded (by making everything dependent on the phallus) and idealised (by making *jouissance* into the closest approximation to the real available to the human subject). The consequence is that it is *feminine* sexuality, despite or because of its apparent mystery, that is taken to be the model for full pleasure, so sexual intercourse comes to represent to the man not so much the *threat* of castration as the *demonstration* of his insufficiency. Bowie (1991, p. 149) suggests that through his use of this imagery of feminine sexuality, Lacan comes close 'to claiming that women, freed from the servitude of the phallus, have already got what men will always crave. Whatever it is that men want to be, women are already there'.

Lacan's theory, in emphasising phallic dominance but also idealising feminine sexuality, might in some respects be incoherent, but it does reflect the experience being referred to in this material on masculine sexuality – the sense that something impossible is being aspired to, and that the failure to achieve it makes the man less powerful than the woman, perhaps dependent upon her. The final element in the quotation from Segal given above, that men often achieve their greatest sexual pleasure through 'experiencing themselves as powerless and submissive', is relevant to this. It suggests that, just as the woman's desire is supposed to be organised around becoming the phallus for the man, so the man's is organised around being *acted upon* by someone fantasised as actually having power – in Lacanian terms, as possessing the phallus herself. Both male and female subjects are thus 'lacking' in relation to the phallus and seek it through their other; but for the man this is given an added poignancy in that it plays with the traditions of power and puts him daringly close to the dependent position which masculinity is organised to avoid. Feminine sexuality is denigrated but also idealised as something immensely pleasurable and overwhelming; in fantasy, the man gives himself up to it in order to become part of it; but he is also terrified as it puts him in contact with his own insufficiency.

All this makes the issue of domination ever more complex and problematic. Benjamin (1988, p. 52) claims that, 'Domination begins with the attempt to deny dependency', so it is not a positive in its own right – like masculinity itself, it is defined negatively, against that which it is not. Perhaps the two processes, domination and dependency, are linked in part like this: to dominate, dependency must be kept at bay; but in sex, there is a recognition by the other which is needed as part of the domination, and the woman can always deny this to the man. There is, indeed, a dual dependency in sex: to have pleasure oneself, to pleasure the other – to be the object of the other's desire. Lacan's (1958, p. 81) formula is again apposite here: 'for each partner in the relation, the subject and the Other, it is not enough to be the subjects of need, nor objects of love, but they must stand as the cause of desire'. Not being desired, not being 'successful' in generating the woman's *jouissance*, is a failure of masculine domination. 'The failure to satisfy women': this is perhaps one of the most forceful indictments of masculine power. Moreover, if Segal is right that men often desire passivity in the sexual encounter, that they want to be done to more than to be doers, then something else is being undermined in the sphere of domination. Men dominate, for sure, but in fantasy they are dependent on the other – and awareness of this dependency makes their domination both more determined and more insecure.

There are two related elements to explore here in rather more detail: first, that of men's difficulties with dependence; secondly, the sense of degradation which, for men, seems often to accompany sex. What was suggested above is that sex places men in a dependent position that undermines the ideology of masculine autonomy and domination. This is due partly to the familiar paradox that 'the master needs the slave', or else he is no longer master – needs recognition from the dominated one if his mastery is to mean anything. It is also, however, that men's sexual enjoyment is often organised around passivity, making the other 'master': 'Men's fantasies, desires and experiences of sex in actual relationships with women are not, it seems, so very different from women's in terms of images of submission – presumably recalling pre-pubescent fantasies in both sexes' (Segal, 1990, p. 214). For men, however, this actuality of sex is a difficult one with which to deal.

What has been emphasised so far is the way in which sex faces men with the distance between the fantasy of possession of the phallus and the experience of insufficiency and inability to 'stand as the cause of desire' for the sexual partner. This calls into question the basis upon which the autonomy of masculine identity is built: as self-sufficient and powerful, able to control and dominate the other. Switching to a somewhat different set of theoretical terms, derived from Kleinian and object relations psychoanalysis, this relates to a broader sense in which sex is a threat to masculine autonomy. Sexuality generates and is built around relationships characterised by dependence. This is true even in the most sadistic of

contacts: the search for the recognition of the other is that much more desperate, the need to prove oneself separate and in control is so much more out
of control. In a reciprocally sado-masochistic relationship, the confusions
of mastery and dependence are even more pronounced (see Benjamin,
1988). And in 'ordinary', non-abusive sex, dependence on the other for
pleasure and for a pleasured response is acute, intense, and paramount.

For men, the dependency generated by sex is a problem, because it
contradicts the ideological basis on which masculine socialisation takes place.

> It is in forsaking our own needs that we prove we have the self-control
> that makes our masculinity secure ... our sexuality connects to our
> sense of masculinity and remains at some deep structure in the culture
> identified with the animal or the 'beastly'. Our sense of our lives can be
> so fragmented that sexual feelings can easily be identified as 'weakness',
> as giving in to temptation.
>
> (Seidler, 1989, pp. 45–7)

Like all obsessional structures, phallic masculinity is maintained in place
by intense scrutiny of its own boundaries, repudiating anything that
threatens to be difficult to assimilate into its already established structures.
Rationality and self-control in this sense go together as aspects of
masculine mastery: in both cases, they treat experience as controllable and
homogeneous, amenable to domination and to the power of the will.
Masculine ideology idealises the life of the rational mind, fetishising
organised activity: moving forward, making progress, thrusting with force
into the future, untrammelled by emotion, liberated from the confusions of
womanly feeling, balanced, critical, self-assertive, free. In masculinist
thought, the body is what holds us back, keeps us in the muddle of nature;
the body is what is *par excellence* feminine, to be seen and owned, but not
to be intrinsic to us.

The gains for men lie in the apparent freedom this repudiation of the
body gives us from the constraints and ties of nature and of our own
subjectivity – as superman, we can master everything. Grosz, summarising
Irigaray's views on the 'specular', comments:

> the masculine can speak of and for the feminine largely because it has
> emptied itself of any relation to the male body, its specificity, and
> socio-political existence ... It gains the illusion of self-distance, the
> illusion of a space of pure reflection, through the creation of a mirroring
> surface that duplicates, re-presents everything *except* itself.
>
> (Grosz, 1990, p. 173)

The 'body' here is something that, through its materiality and specificity,
demands that the abstractions of 'pure thought' are abandoned and that
something muddled, messy and uncontrollable is allowed into the
symbolisation of experience. One central attribute of masculinist ideology,

it is claimed here, is to oppose 'the body' in this sense, and the emotion associated with it, in order to perpetuate domination – to maintain the obsessional structures of control. Through avoidance of emotion, through passionless enterprise, men can always make the best, the most rational, the most 'objective' decisions, least influenced by the unnecessary contaminations of personal desire and inconsistent subjectivity. (And, of course, we can give ourselves up to the demands of production and profit, but that is another story.)

This renunciation of the body and of emotion, however, carries with it a very high cost. 'We lose any sense of *grounding* ourselves in our own embodied experience as we identify our sense of masculinity with being objective and impartial', writes Seidler (1989, p. 129). Where men claim to be separate from the body, the body is repressed: men act as if we do not know it, as if it has no part in our experience. Moreover, with an ideology based on an objectifying trajectory, it ceases to be possible to adequately construe the self – to make sense of one's own experience of uncertainty and emotional confusion. This is an important aspect of the situation of creating 'a mirroring surface that duplicates, re-presents everything *except* itself' – men's own experience is left unconstruable because masculinity is based on its repression. Self-control, mastery of nature and of our nature, is a defining marker of the masculine state. Consequently, when the repressed returns, when for example the body makes its mark through sex, it is experienced as a failure, as a dangerous act of giving in to the bestial elements in our make-up.

All this means that sex is both dangerously 'basic' and also somehow external – not part of what defines the man as 'man', as that advanced creature of rational mastery. Sex is always there, an obsession, but it is not part of us; being repudiated and repressed, it paradoxically threatens to take control. Seidler (1991, p. 86) comments from a man's perspective that, 'We have been brought up to be ashamed of our sexual feelings, though often at the same time obsessed with them'. This experience reflects a massive shaft of metaphorical connections, linking the body, sex, nature, women and the fear of femininity. Constantly threatening to break up the tangled yet fragile structures of masculine identity, sex is fascinating and frightening, something that makes it possible for men to be dependent yet also raises all the anxieties of failure, dissolution and loss of control described above. It represents a channel of personal 'truth', because it seems to contain the possibility of having intention, premeditation and self-consciousness overwhelmed by passion, yet it is disturbing for precisely that same reason – that the self, with its obsessionally embraced masculine armour, may be lost. Sexuality thus becomes relegated to the category of the bestial in man – rather like madness, perhaps – producing its characteristic response of fascination and fear.

The projection into sexuality of associations of bestiality is linked with a reason–nature or science–nature dichotomy which is itself ineluctably gendered, and which starts to move us back to the issue of sexual violence. Nature is constructed as female, and this has consequences.

> Underneath the image of nature in modern science as passive and entirely knowable is a suppressed signifier of nature as the ultimate force, capable of wreaking havoc over mind and culture. It contains intimations of something which always resists being fully known (like woman) and fully controlled (like woman) – else why the emphasis on pursuit and control?
>
> (Hollway, 1989, p. 115)

To the extent that sex is absorption in the body, involving giving up self-control and overcoming inhibition of desire, to the extent that it invokes '*jouissance*', it represents the return of the repressed – of nature and all its feminine flows. The body-armour of the man falls away, is itself penetrated by the fantasised and repudiated femininity of boundary-less, unbound energy – with all its threats of devastation and havoc. 'All that's solid melts into air': the body's return is one that sweeps away the control on which masculine mastery is based.

There is a pattern of causality present here, in which the signifier 'sex' sets up signifieds that undermine the culture of masculinity as it has evolved over the centuries, producing in men terror, shame, a sense of failure, and – inevitably – anger and a drive to retribution. If we cannot tame the body, we can at least hit back at the body's representative, the woman. This is all culturally given: 'masculinity' equals rationality, 'femininity' equals nature/body; sex is the overcoming of the former by the latter, hence is unbearable and disowned. But it raises the question of how, in the life of each individual man, this algebra becomes experience; that is, of what the developmental processes are through which masculine sexuality becomes delimited and channelled in these particular, and potentially destructive, ways. In contemporary psychoanalysis, this question is generally answered in terms of object relationships, beginning with the first relationship of all.

DESIRE AND THE MOTHER

For the man, writes Olivier:

> what is at issue in sexual love is the re-enactment of his earliest love relation, that with his mother . . . hence the seriousness of impotence for the man: it both prevents him from taking possession of the second woman and signifies that he is not yet separated from the first, the forbidden mother.
>
> (Olivier, 1980, p. 99)

The first relationship, the 'earliest love relation', assumed to be with the mother, is often conceptualised in psychoanalysis as if it is something outside culture. The pre-Oedipal world is pictured as one in which there is direct absorption of the infant in the mother without mediation by the third term of the Oedipal progression (me–mummy–daddy; self–other–law). In contrast to the distancing and constructing power of this third term, the way (as Lacanians might put it) the Symbolic order determines the positioning of the individual human subject and the way language constructs identity, the first relationship is theorised as something of the body, absorbing and 'symbiotic'. Developmentally speaking, this is an impossible relationship, consisting of complete oneness with the other yet holding in it the potential for, even the first moment of, separation. This is, in effect, the Lacanian Real which can never be encountered, the state before any boundary is marked between subject and object. In Kristeva's (1983) terms, it might even be before the moment of 'abjection', when the subject catches a glimmer of awareness of the gap between self and other, and is overwhelmed by the horror of disappearing into that abyss. Empirically, perhaps, we are speaking in Kleinian terms here, of the investment of desire in a bodily space, of an experiential world full to overflowing with anxiety and love, bounded desperately by the struggles of the psyche to survive. Jacobus (1990, p. 160), articulating precisely the loss of language that occurs when one seeks the origin of development, when one tries to conceive of the experience of being 'conceived', of being alive but still absorbed in the mother's whole, comments: 'One response to the current return to Klein: it feels like eating one's words'.

Eating one's words: that which structures I and you, subject and object, disappears into a space of oneness in which there are no differentiations. This is 'thinking through the body', the feminine mode again (Gallop, 1988), supposedly opposed to, or subversive of, the rational and controlling use of language characteristic of masculinity. We are back here with Grunberger's (1989) notion of the 'monad', discussed in Chapter 2, the post-natal continuation of pre-natal oneness, in which the baby experiences her or himself as still perfectly linked with the mother. Grunberger identifies the monad as a preserver of infantile sanity in the face of the assaults of the post-natal environment; but it is also a continuing pull backwards during development, a source of regressive narcissism as a fantasised solution to all problems presented by reality. For Grunberger, along with Chasseguet-Smirgel (1975) and others, the opposition is a gendered one between Narcissus and Oedipus, with the former identified as a maternal principle of oneness, an unattainable fantasy, and the latter as an encounter with paternal reality – the reality of the world as it is. Engaging with the conflicts of Oedipus is engaging with difference, with how the world is actually structured and with the necessity for toleration of constraint and uncertainty; resisting Oedipus, staying with the fantasy of the maternal monad, is narcissistic regression, wanting everything pure, whole, and uncontaminated.

Amongst the various issues which could be taken up here, some of which have been discussed in Chapter 2, one concerns a gendered dispute over the nature of anality. For Grunberger (1989), anality opposes narcissism, which tends towards a fantasy of purity and which is consequently opposed to corporeality and toleration of the messy nature of reality. In this account, anything that pursues purity and despises anality – despises the real dirt and confusion of the world – is regressively narcissistic, possibly fascistically so. It operates by refusing conflict, denying heterogeneity, making what is different out of bounds, the object of aggressive assault. This kind of regressiveness enforces rigid, envious values; it fights only for itself, staving off experience of the world, because heterogeneity and complexity cannot be borne. 'The triumph of narcissism over anality means not only an apparent liberation from Oedipus and from conflict, but also a liberation from reality – or, in a phrase, from the human condition' (Grunberger, 1989, p. 155). In this version of development, anality is a positive move towards reality.

The identification of narcissism with life-denying rejection of experience, symbolised in the first instance as anality and then as the Oedipus complex, offers some helpful insights into the psychodynamics of various states of rigidity, for instance racism and fascism (see Grunberger, 1979; Frosh, 1989). But the added association of this state of mind with the maternal principle is a confusing and disconcerting one, at odds both with the theories described earlier and with observations of masculine character-armour and the way it develops in the face of the multiplicity and heterogeneity of cultural experience. It is possible to argue, as Grunberger does, that what is going on here is a regressive response to the fantasy of the female principle (absorption in the mother), but even in this view femininity itself is flowing, not static, in that it breaks down boundaries and unsettles the received distinctions between self and other. Grunberger chooses to read this maternal union as a denial of difference, as everything is absorbed in one whole; but one might just as easily construe it as a refusal to accept rigid boundaries and phallic dominance. Olivier picks up some of the sexual politics here in the following riposte to the superiority of anality over the mother, which refuses to accept that anality is life-enhancing, as Grunberger claims.

> The man's anal game comes down to this: how to stop the other from existing; how to remove all trace of her desire; how to kill her in fantasy.
> (Olivier, 1980, p. 64)

There is more than a disagreement here, there is a radical difference of interpretation of what constitutes 'reality', and of the extent to which the masculine order – the Oedipus, if it must be – can be tolerated. For the man, the choices apparently forced by reality are necessary; for the woman, they are ways of exerting control.

Perhaps the most coherent critique of the Grunberger and Chasseguet-Smirgel version of the dynamics of regressive narcissism comes from Benjamin (1988). Indeed, this critique leads into a statement of the inadequacy of all Oedipal theory, that is, theory which takes the traditional model of the Oedipal encounter with the father as *the* primary symbol of maturity and ability to live with reality. Developmentally, the Oedipus complex is supposed to offer to the child (specifically here, the *male* child, an important point in relation to the critique of this peculiarly masculinist rendering of psychoanalytic theory) an encounter with something outside the mother which is terrifying and yet which offers an object of identification that aids the child in discovering his own autonomy and strength. Benjamin notes that in Freud's thought this is a complex and ambivalent procedure:

> Paternal authority ... is not merely rooted in the rational law that forbids incest and patricide, but also in the erotics of ideal love, the guilty identification with power that undermines the son's desire for freedom.
>
> (Benjamin, 1988, p. 148)

Versions of the Oedipus complex that stress the encounter with rationality and oppose it to the 'irrationality' of (feminine) narcissism and the regressive pull to the mother, articulate only part of the full dynamic. Effectively, they idealise the father as representative of reality and split off the fantastic and disturbing features of the paternal threat, projecting them into the figure of the mother, who thus becomes further denigrated. As Benjamin points out, not only does this produce a misogynistic account of development congruent with masculine repudiation of femininity, but it is also bad theory in its own terms.

> Paradoxically, the image of the liberating father undermines the acceptance of difference that the Oedipus complex is meant to embody. For the idea of the father as protection against 'limitless narcissism' at once authorises his idealisation and the mother's denigration ... Difference turns out to be governed by the code of domination.
>
> (*ibid.*, p. 135)

This is no way to come to terms with difference; rather, it is a means by which the possibility of co-existing differences is denied. There is only one way, the way of the father; the seeds of fascism seem just as likely to inhere in this as in the other view.

If there can be no easy acceptance of the maternal–paternal axis as narcissism–progression, it does contribute to the difficult task of offering some account of early development that might aid in understanding the power of the myth of the destructive female. The argument concerning masculine development goes like this. Freud (e.g. 1933) was wrong in thinking that feminine development is the harder path, a mistake generated by his failure to look far enough back from the Oedipus complex. Certainly, if one takes the Oedipal view, one has to explain how the girl shifts her object of desire from the mother to the father. But this makes gender development contingent on the nature of the *object*, when it makes more sense to see it in terms of the *subject*, in particular of the identifications around which subjectivity is constructed. Looking at the pre-Oedipal period one is impressed not so much with the directions in which the infant expresses her or his desire, but with the incorporations, internalisations and identifications which she or he demonstrates – the psychological procedures, modelled on bodily ones, that build up the ego by taking in material from outside. Seen like this, it is masculinity which is the more precarious achievement. Incorporation of the mother is the natural position for all infants – the first relationship – making identification with femininity easy; indeed, object relations theorists suggest that it is so easy that girls and women consistently show difficulties in becoming separate (e.g. Eichenbaum and Orbach, 1982). Releasing oneself from the mother and finding a father with whom to identify, on the other hand, is a task much more difficult to achieve, yet this is the boy's task, at least under social conditions in which gender development and self-development go hand in hand.

Putting a Lacanian gloss on it, Ragland-Sullivan expresses the problem for the boy as follows:

> Lacan points to the exceptional anxiety involved in taking on a masculine identification. Indeed, the figure of the male *qua* male might be called the cultural lie which maintains that sexual identity can be personified by making difference itself a position.
>
> (Ragland-Sullivan, 1991, p. 51)

Masculinity constructs itself on the basis of a separation from that which the infant knows – the mother and all her feminine power. Defined in this way as separation, as difference, masculine identity is perpetuated by a continuing process of shutting out the feminine, of 'linking identity, discourse and sexual apparatus to a fantasy of superiority *qua* difference' (Ragland-Sullivan, 1991, p. 59). Masculinity thus has no secure base of its own, no positive content, but is rather premised only on the exclusion of the other – a position which is bound to be uncertain, always in danger of collapsing under the force of the fantasised plenitude of femininity. Thus, the negation of the feminine, its exclusion, is a defensive response to the fantasy that femininity is the positive pole, and that masculinity is defined only by difference. In this lies a reversal indeed.

It is worth considering the developmental details of what might happen here. There is, at first, a tremendously powerful bond, an absorption of the infant in the mother, an almost-oneness, infused with anxieties (if the Kleinians are right), something of the body, relatively unmediated, but perhaps already marked with the horror of potential dissolution. Girls have many problems with this – of differentiation, of finding a place which is both bodily and yet autonomous, of entering the world of symbols, of becoming true subjects in their own right. But they also have available an identificatory object offering a positive content for femininity, even if this is often or usually vitiated by the mother's internalised negative self-image, provoked by the oppressions of gender devaluation. For boys, attaining masculinity is a striving towards something unknown and unknowable: a state of difference from the mother, yet grounded in her. The trend of early experience is to suck the boy in, to make him fused with the mother; but as fused, he cannot master her, cannot take on the vague but intensely felt promise of phallic mastery, cannot conquer nature – his own or hers. Consequently, his activity is directed towards repudiation of the mother, a repudiation helped both by her own fantasy of him as other, as separate from her (hence a potential object of desire, because not the same, not already owned), and also by the Oedipal fantasy that the masculine order dominates the feminine, that the boy can grow into a phallus of his own.

The notion that the Oedipal fascination with the father (Oedipal both in the developmental sense and as a reference to a certain kind of theory) may actually be a defensive manoeuvre whereby the boy deals with his terror of, as well as his (more conventionally recognised) desire for, his mother, is one that is stressed in contemporary psychoanalytic writing from a number of theoretical standpoints. Benjamin, for example, ties together many threads in the following passage:

> Paternal recognition has a defensive aspect; with it the child denies dependency and dissociates himself from his previous maternal tie. The father's entry is a kind of *deus ex machina* that solves the insoluble conflict of rapprochement, the conflict between the desire to hold onto the mother, and the desire to fly away. The child wants to solve this problem by becoming independent without the experience of loss. And the 'solution' to this dilemma is to split – to assign the contradictory strivings to different parents. Schematically, the mother can become the object of desire, the father the subject of desire in whom one recognises oneself. Separation-individuation thus becomes a gender issue, and recognition and independence are now organised within the frame of gender.
>
> (Benjamin, 1988, p. 104)

The boy turns away from the mother and identifies with the father, representing the world; but this process is so infused with anxiety (the kind of anxiety reflected in theories of regressive narcissism) that father and mother are split into paternal and maternal 'principles', the one idealised, the other devalued. 'The phallus', writes Benjamin (1988, p. 123), 'acquires its power as a defensive reaction to maternal power and as an element of excitement that contrasts with her holding and containment.' Just as Oedipal theory idealises the father and thus fails to confront the central challenge of difference, so the boy child takes on the mantle of masculinity through a process that cannot tolerate the actual ambiguity of both father and mother, but instead invests in the one at the expense of the other.

The Lacanian rendering of this same developmental dynamic clearly partakes of the traditional Oedipal imagery of denigrated mother and idealised father. Thus, the mother (or, as Felman [1987, p. 104] suggests, the mother's *image*) is conceptualised as standing in an imaginary relationship to the evolving infant subject, in which there is an absorption of the subject in a mirroring process that is essentially narcissistic. In contrast, the father – or at least his word or 'name' – represents a principle both of separation and of the inclusion of the subject in the Symbolic order.

> The paternal metaphor diagrams the child's entry into the symbolic order and the social world beyond the family structure, as regulated by the other. The paternal metaphor names the child and thus positions it so that it can be replaced discursively by the 'I', in order to enter language as a speaking being.
>
> (Grosz, 1990, p. 104)

This process involves denigration of the mother – 'The child can only accede to the paternal metaphor by acknowledging (maternal) castration or privation' (*ibid.*). In addition, by presenting entry into the Symbolic order as a step which is *necessary* for mental health (otherwise there is only psychosis), it implicitly suggests that the paternal influence is of a more advanced developmental kind than the maternal one. Yet, as has been described above, Lacanian theory also points to the *insecurity* of masculinity, the way what seems to be an advance towards ownership of some concrete power is actually experienced as a step into vacuousness, a masquerade all of its own.

The boy seems to be promised the phallus, a promise apparently made concrete in all the demonstrations of masculine domination to be found in the outside world, but the phallus is never actually to be his. As discussed earlier, the phallus is itself fraudulent; there is no mastery that is complete. The boy knows this from his own experience already, but cannot bear it.

> The father's phallus stands for the wholeness and separateness that the child's real helplessness and dependency belie ... The devaluation of the need for the other becomes a touchstone of adult masculinity.
>
> (Benjamin, 1988, p. 171)

Hunting for a centre for his masculinity, the boy looks towards the father;

but what he discovers is that while masculinity presents an appearance of integration and strength, its inner coordinates will always remain mysterious and unavailable to articulation. Instead, masculinity comes to be defined experientially as a movement *away* from something – from maternal intimacy and dependence – rather than towards something with a clear and vibrant content of its own. Masculinity's apparent strength, its attractiveness for the boy, is all on the outside, which is why so much energy tends to go into shoring it up.

It is specifically the mother who is repudiated, and through this repudiation the boy turns his back on the intense contact with the other that she represents. Because of the precariousness of his own sense of mastery, he must battle continually to assert himself against her, against the feminine principle of oneness, against what has the opprobrium of 'regressive narcissism'. It is only in relation to difference from the mother that the boy can form a relationship with his own masculine identity; experiencing her power and fearing that it will take him over, he looks away from her to the promise of the phallus, but finds only empty space. Benjamin spells out the impact of this process on the boy's capacity for intimacy and dependence.

> The boy's repudiation of femininity is the central thread of the Oedipus complex, no less important than the renunciation of the mother as a love object. To be feminine like her would be a throwback to the preoedipal dyad, a dangerous regression ... To the extent that identification is blocked, the boy has no choice but to overcome his infancy by repudiation of dependency.
>
> (Benjamin, 1988, p. 162)

It is this association of the mother with dependency that, in this account, so deeply affects the boy's capacity to form intimate relationships with others, and hence converts his sexuality into something which has to be used defensively, as an attribute of mastery and an expression of rage, rather than as a link with the other. 'Never again to be caught in the same place, in the same desire as the woman', writes Olivier (1980, p. 41), 'this is the main driving force of the man's misogyny.' The powerful injunction against being the same as the woman produces a confusion in which all 'womanly' attributes are rendered problematic, made into something 'other'.

Sexually, the boy learns to fear his desire, because it brings back the loss of mastery. Converting it into conquest and performance, it becomes 'an individual achievement that reflects upon the position of a man within the pecking order of masculinity' (Seidler, 1989, p. 39), a way of establishing oneself rather than making contact with another. Intimacy is potentially dangerous, because the boundaries of the masculine self are so fragile that they can be all too easily overwhelmed. Paradoxically, this explains the apparent rigidity of so much masculinity: one cannot bend at all, for fear of falling apart. It also produces the vicious splitting of the feminine in male fantasy – the madonna/whore division that parcels out the safe sphere of nurture from the demonic sphere of the erotic, with its accompanying imagery of devouring and being devoured. As he gets close to her, so the man is faced with the potential loss of his identity; sexual rage is never far away. Most poignantly, when faced with female desire, the male backs off. 'In the end, the woman's strong desire to take, to have . . . triggers in the man the fear of being possessed, robbed, trapped' (Olivier, 1980, p. 85). Instead of the man accepting and being at one with his own sexual subjectivity, he sees the idealised and feared woman as the locus of sexual desire, as that which produces it. The woman consequently embodies both exciting and disturbing elements of sexuality, becoming something to be feared and controlled. This pushes into place, once again, the drive to be master, to survive dissolution by maintaining control.

ABUSE AGAIN

This brings the story back to domination. Here is Benjamin's summary statement:

> The vulnerability of masculinity that is forged in the crucible of femininity, the 'great task' of separation that is so seldom completed, lays the groundwork for the later objectification of women. The mother stands as the prototype of the undifferentiated object. She serves men as their other, their counterpart, the side of themselves they repress.
>
> (Benjamin, 1988, p. 77)

Why do men sexually abuse women and children? If there is any validity to the analysis presented above, sexual abuse is a function of men's own abhorrence of the feminine within – it is a kind of continuing assault on the body of the mother. In both forms of abuse, the nexus is one of hostility/rage/sexuality (see MacLeod and Sarraga, 1988), centring on that splitting-off of sex from intimacy which is a crucial element in masculine sexual socialisation. Women are the primary recipients of the offshoots of this splitting: 'If women are not enough of a problem in their own right, they become so in their role as the bearers or symbolic representatives of various disavowed, warded off, unacceptable aspects of men' (Fogel, 1986, quoted in Segal, 1990, p. 75). The man's rage as he experiences sexual desire, associated with a breaking down of masculinity and a sucking back into the body of the powerful mother, is extruded onto the woman, who is, both individually and socially, the sanctioned recipient of violence. The growing strength of women and the declining power of traditional masculine modes of character organisation (declining through the dismantling of old authority structures, the disbanding of traditional and reliable work environments, and the general heterogeneity of contemporary capitalism – see Seidler, 1991) reinforce this rage, now more like an infantile despair at the loss of power than the fully formed expression of mastery.

But why should children be abused? There are some persuasive descriptive accounts of the pathways to abuse, for example in Finkelhor (1984); also some which link powerfully with feminist analyses of gender relationships (e.g. MacLeod and Sarraga, 1988). The important culturally mediated association of children with sexuality should also not be denied, even though it often is (see Glaser and Frosh, 1993). But here, let us keep to the implications of the earlier analysis of masculine development. Renouncing the mother and striving for the father, but also living in the exquisitely painful consciousness of the impossibility of attaining the phallus – of being truly rational and masterful – the male has only a fragile armour of masculinity, kept in place by repression of emotion, desire and intimate connection with others. Sex, then, becomes a tremendously important channel for the expression of emotion, which is denied any other channel; but it is also a terrifying threat. This is because it makes the man dependent on the other and also represents the potential overwhelming of rational control by erratic desire. Masculine sexuality may then, if alienated enough, seek the least threatening, the most controllable of objects – which may not be the adult woman. As Olivier points out, having to deal with the desire of the other/mother is terrifying to the man, because it carries with it the threat of fusion, of being sucked back into her narcissistic womb and thus losing all the laboriously built boundaries of masculinity: 'There is no greater threat to the man than the express desire of the woman, which for him invariably takes on the form of an evil trap (evil because linked to the desire of the all-powerful mother)' (1980, p. 96). Searching for a more controllable object, one which can be silenced, forced, made in fantasy into anything at all, some men alight upon a child.

Of course not all men abuse children, and the differences between those who do and those who do not are crucial for theory and therapeutic practice. These differences may arise from a number of sources: the quality of early relationships as well as of those formed during adulthood; challenges to emotional distancing faced during development; differences in patterns of gender socialisation; and specific experiences of trauma or reparation. Presumably, it is the extent to which such specific experiences enable a man to deal with the potential splitting of intimacy and dependence from sexuality, and hence the degree to which he can come to a more integrated absorption of maternal and paternal images, that is the primary determinant of his capacity to overcome sexual rage and use sex for contact rather than control. In addition, socially induced patterns of powerlessness and privation are crucial mediators of the propensity to abuse and rape (see Segal, 1990, for a subtle discussion of this point). But most abusers of children are men, and this requires explanation. The suggestion here is that the systematic links are given not only through the organisation of society along patriarchal lines, but also in the more micro-cosmic patterns of masculine sexual socialisation. The painful mixture of impulse and over-control, of separation and intimacy, of fear and desire – this mixture so common in men is also something that infiltrates men's relationships with children, sometimes leading to abuse. As sex is the only form of intimacy allowable to many men, all intimacy tends to turn into sex; as emotion is so linked with mastery and power, so threatening to it, then power is used where emotion would be more appropriate; as nurture is so feared, it is renounced, denied, and in the end brutalised. This is not true of all men, of course not. But this is what all men struggle with, at least while our experience is so pervasively, so relentlessly gendered.

SEX AND SEXUALITY

Sex, therefore, is not all there is to sexuality. Sexuality is a broader term, carrying with it a heavy baggage of connections with identity, with socialisation and with culture. The manner in which we understand masculinity influences the manner in which we understand masculine sexuality; sexuality is a psychological entity, not just a set of biological urges or behavioural techniques. The formulation given here suggests that the separation of sex from sexuality, a separation characteristic of much sex therapy, is itself part of the ideology of masculinity, making sex decontextualised, isolated from the dangers of emotion and boundary dissolution. Success and failure: these are the terms of alienation in any discussion of what sex means – it becomes something out there, to be achieved or performed, a mark of mastery.

The seeds of masculine sexuality are embedded deeply in relationships, both concretely and figuratively. Currently, they are to be found in domination and fear, in ambivalence towards intimacy, in a desire for an other who both is and is not the mother, and in awareness of the space that a father might fill. They are to be found, too, in a cultural order built around fantasies of wholeness and rational perfection, safe from dissolution but also bereft of emotion; and they are to be found in certain kinds of specific family relationships in which asymmetry and denial of femininity are structuring dimensions. For psychotherapists, all this suggests the need for exploration of the significance of sex in the life of male clients; in the context of abuse, it means a challenge to all manifestations of domination and force. Most of all, it means opposition to that splitting, that fearful turning away, seen so often when men's emotional life is the issue. Rationality, mastery, control: exploration of masculine sexuality is as much about these issues as it is about sexual 'performance'. Focusing only on the latter is, indirectly or directly, a masculinist strategy; it says, 'this far will I go, but I will not really challenge what is, not really try to make the differences speak'.

Chapter 6

Transgressing sexual difference

SPEAKING WITHOUT WORDS

I have been seeing Mr and Mrs A. together for couple therapy for fourteen months. In the middle of one session, Mr A. speaks for just over fifteen minutes on the history of his complaint. In the course of this speech, which is eloquent and evocative, he mentions his wife only once, when he notes that his first encounter with therapy was before he met her, twenty years ago. He says he is thinking of writing a novel about his experiences and has started drafting it. When he has finished I ask his wife for her response. She says she has none, then that she speaks only to herself and does not share her feelings with others. Then she begins to cry, unexpectedly, without warning, automatically, as if to herself, uncontrollably. She says, 'Nobody . . .'. The complete sentence, it turns out later, is 'Nobody would be interested.' Her husband and I sit speechless, wrapped in different reveries of our own. Mine concerns my investment in an unconscious alliance with Mr A. which is constructed on the basis of exclusion of his wife. When an alliance is formed in a three-person system, there will always be an excluded term, and it is clearly no accident that here it is the woman who is left out. She cries and we watch; I want to make a comment on this process of exclusion, weave something insightful and connecting into the isolation which is being experienced. But Mrs A.'s tears tear this shapeless fabric, creating a rent through which words only fall. We sit in silence until she is able to speak; she then says, 'Sorry'.

In Mrs. A's tears, in her 'Nobody' and in her 'Sorry', there is a set of questions being asked about transference, countertransference and concern. What is it in the situation that is evoking for her an isolation and powerlessness which she has always experienced, but which she has so far avoided articulating in therapy? Is it the specific situation of her invisibility in her husband's narrative – married for twenty years, but no longer (if ever) thought about? Or is it the generality and genderedness of the two-against-one, the men who collude in not recognising or knowing her? Why do her tears, after all no unfamiliar phenomenon in therapy, create such a strong sense of rupture, of a dead space into which spoken words will fall unheard? Is it that she cannot speak because the conditions for speech have not been established, the main condition being, straightforwardly, a guarantee of a listener, of somewhere for her own words to go? So that at this moment of therapy, there is for her only the conviction that nobody is interested, that her voice is excluded by the narrative structure of masculine language; again straightforwardly, that only the man will be heard.

Or are her tears a kind of temptation or strategy, a bid for a space in which to speak, couched in a non-linguistic form in order to subvert language, to demonstrate its inadequacy? By crying without words, she silences all speech in the room, then can take her time to formulate retrospectively what it is that she wants her tears to mean. Her physical, non-verbal punctuation of the discussion could then be seen as a powerful and somewhat nihilistic intervention in which the ordinary, if emotive, use of language is destroyed. With this occurrence, the progression of the therapy through time is stopped: we can only wait while the crying goes on. A barrier or boundary is placed between the historical account in Mr A.'s narrative and what happens next; a pause which is also a space.

All this raises a broad question which is the topic for this chapter: the question of who is inside and who outside of language, who has what kind of mastery and how this is expressed in gendered terms in the context of therapy. In the last two chapters, the way in which phallic authority is embedded in language and subjectivity has been explored, amid an application of both Lacanian and Kleinian theory to the construction of masculine sexuality. One of the strongest elements in this is the manner in which femininity is theorised as outside, or rather as the boundary of, the masculine condition, as that border against which it tests and reassures itself. Femininity in that sense marks a space within which the masculine moves; speech is marked by the existence of something outside speech, which defines its limits. Moving on from this work, I want to take up some ideas articulated by Julia Kristeva to explore further the nature of this boundary, and to argue that the relatively conventional distinction between 'masculine time' and 'feminine space' can be used to construct a model of the way in which therapy is penetrated by sexual difference. This model might also start to show some ways in which the impasses produced by this situation can be overcome.

SUBJECT AND OBJECT

In a passage in 'Women's Time', Kristeva makes the following comment on sexual difference:

Sexual difference . . . is translated by and translates a difference in the relationship of subjects to the symbolic contract which *is* the social contract: a difference, then, in the relationship to power, language and meaning.

(Kristeva, 1979, p. 196)

At first glance, this is a relatively linear, straightforward statement in its presentation of the standard feminist insight that power and gender intersect. It seems to say that sexual difference is *equivalent to* ('is translated by and translates') a difference of position within the social/symbolic world, so generating a difference in experience. But Kristeva's sentence is also full of the codes of Lacanian-influenced psychoanalysis. The signifiers 'translation', 'symbolic', 'language', 'meaning', even 'difference' create an associative flow in which sexual difference becomes linked to a division in language, so governing a difference in the production of meaning.

What exactly is this difference? Simply put, one would have thought it to be one of exclusion, of subject and object – of who is allowed to speak and who is spoken about, but has no voice of her own. In the history of patriarchal culture, this by definition means the exclusion of the woman. Man speaks for woman, about woman, naming and placing her and not allowing her her subjecthood, denying her ownership of her own position and voice. Instead, through the processes outlined in the previous chapter, she is idealised and denigrated, made into an object of representation and investigation. This is in part what Lacan (1972–3, p. 144) is commenting on in his famous slogan, 'There is no such thing as *The* Woman'. Speaking more fully of this absence, Lacan claims that the essentially patriarchal organisation of culture, or properly speaking the phallic structuring of language, means that woman takes up her place as the Other, as something which stands outside the Symbolic as its negative, giving it its presence through her exclusion. Provocatively, Lacan claims that this is also the insight of feminists: that is, that all he is doing is putting into theoretical form the complaint made by women who feel themselves to be placed outside of language, to be left out of the corridors of power. In so doing, Lacan dramatises the process whereby men take over women's positions, speaking for women all the time, even when what is being said is that they are not being allowed to speak.

> There is woman only as excluded by the nature of things, which is the nature of words, and it has to be said that if there is one thing they themselves are complaining about enough at the moment it is well and truly that – only they don't know what they are saying, which is all the difference between them and me.

(Lacan 1972–3, p. 144)

Lacan is saying that he can speak for women because they have no ability to speak for themselves, because they are excribed from language, excluded, other. Indeed, the definition of 'woman' seems here to be 'she who is outside language' ('the nature of things, which is the nature of words') – because if she was 'inside' language, owning it, she would be man. And Lacan can articulate this knowingly, because he *is* inside langauge, master of it; women can only act their exclusion out.

This is all a fairly clear manifestation of sexual difference as seen by Kristeva, a 'difference in the relationship to power, language and meaning'. Indeed, Lacan makes the 'difference' even more pronounced, apparently insisting on the impossibility of resistance and empowerment. Being excluded from language, women cannot know what they are saying, even when they complain about their exclusion. Consequently, when Kristeva theorises about how sexual difference 'is translated by and translates a difference in the relationship of subjects to the symbolic contract which is the social contract', she cannot know what she is saying – that her own alienation is what is at stake. Additionally, later, when she writes that 'the social contract ... is based on an essentially sacrificial relationship of separation and articulation of differences' (Kristeva, 1979, p. 199), she herself is being placed in the position of having to make the sacrifice -- or, rather, of becoming the sacrificial lamb. Women may talk as much as they like, but in this vision of things they cannot, by definition, ever be in command of their own words. And to those who might say that that is true for everyone, men as well as women, there is Lacan's categorical assertion to testify otherwise: 'only they [i.e. women] don't know what they are saying, which is all the difference between them and me'.

The arrogance of this Lacanian claim is quite obvious, and its theoretical incoherence will be described below. But it should be noted that it is not without historical and psychological truth: women have been excluded, consistently and violently, from the male order; and when they have not been quiet about their exclusion, they have been made to suffer. In the Lacanian movement itself, this tableau has been enacted several times, most notably in the prototypical case of Luce Irigaray. Opposing the arrogance of Lacan's self-appointed mastery of femininity, and picking up the performance element in his provocative style, she writes of him:

> The production of ejaculations of all sorts, often prematurely emitted, makes him miss, in the desire for identification with the lady, what her own pleasure might be all about.
> And ... his?
>
> (Irigaray, 1977, p. 91)

Of course the consequence of such an impertinent question – what is Lacan's pleasure? – was to be Irigaray's exclusion from Lacan's school, her sacrifice of her position in the Lacanian sphere. It should be noted, however, that this is not quite because she does not know what she is saying, or even because she speaks and writes in ignorance of the possible effect of her words; she seems quite confident that she has more access than

Lacan to the woman's point of view, and that she knows how to put it into words. Rather, her exclusion derives from a specific masculine strategy of control: too much of women's speech, when it opposes the master, is not to be allowed.

This is the first instance of the obvious tautology of Lacan's position – and that of patriarchy as a whole. Lacan claims that women are by definition excluded from language, that it is impossible in principle for a woman to express herself knowingly in the Symbolic, so becoming a full subject of that order of experience. Then, when a woman does act like that, speaking her mind and using Lacanian rhetoric to puncture his claims (*he* cannot know what *she* wants, but consistently misses her point), Lacan actively excludes her, keeps her at bay. Using a psychoanalytic analogy, it is not that the unconscious has no capacity for expressing itself, quite the contrary; it is the active act of repression that keeps it (relatively) quiet. It is necessary to keep it quiet because, if allowed to speak, the unconscious would have so much to say that it would expose as a sham the claim of consciousness to be all there is to psychic life. The analogy here, between the unconscious and femininity, is an already familiar one to which I will return.

The power of Kristeva's logic and rhetoric offers another relevant example of the transparent fraudulence of Lacan's claim. Kristeva is not quite part of the 'écriture féminine' movement associated for example with Hélène Cixous; rather, as will be argued more fully below, she takes a position on sexual difference in which what might be called feminine and masculine principles are explored in terms of their intertwining and mutual dependence. The order of language which Lacan calls the 'Symbolic' is given great weight in Kristeva's work, but she also argues that a more 'feminine' form, the 'semiotic', is ever-present, existing in relation to the Symbolic order, with each one demanding recognition if the other is to survive. It will be argued below that this formulation is extremely important for possibilities of movement beyond the pessimistic vision of a sexual difference fixed for all time; the point here is that this woman Kristeva is free enough in her own understanding and use of language to add something significant – perhaps even revolutionary – to the scheme of things developed by Lacan. She seems powerful enough here, inscribed in language, using it with force and as her own; there is nothing to suggest that she knows not what she says.

There is another line of reasoning, this time concerning language itself, that seems to make Lacan's claims incoherent. The woman is excluded, has no voice, is other, knows not what she is saying. Yet, in being the negative of the Symbolic she makes it possible for the Symbolic to exist – in having no voice, she articulates a difference that makes speech possible. According to the Lacanian version of Saussurean linguistics, meaning arises only out of difference, as Laplanche and Leclaire explain in a famously lucid treble-negative:

If a signifier refers to a signified, it is only through the mediation of the entire system of signifiers: there is no signifier that does not refer to the absence of others and that is not defined by its position in the system.

(Laplanche and Leclaire, 1966, p. 154)

At its simplest, this promotes a view of language in which what is articulated has its meaning defined by its boundary-conditions: it is only by means of contrast with what is not said that what is said can be known. This in itself is an important enough point, making each signifier dependent upon the whole system of signification for its production of particular signifieds. But there is also something in the tone of this quotation that reveals the source of its dynamic force. In the space of one sentence, there is one 'no', two 'nots' and an 'absence': the negative is startlingly present, keeps raising her hungry head. It is a psychoanalytic truism, beginning with Freud (1925b), that the stronger the negation the more important the truth of what has been negated. So, in the context of this discussion about the negation of femininity, the more absent she is, the more excluded the woman is from language, the more speech seems to depend on her voice. Meaning is produced only by difference; Lacan (1957, p. 154) says he is 'forced to accept the notion' – that is, he does not particularly want to – 'of an incessant sliding of the signified under the signifier'; without the other the whole system falls apart. From all the parallel lines of allusion and denial, what seems to come across is a rather different relationship of femininity to power from that presented by Lacan. Not just historically, in terms of her reproductive function, but also continually, in terms of her impact on the whole order of things – Symbolic as well as Imaginary – the woman makes the masculine exist.

This vision of the woman who is no longer excluded naturally, but who is kept at bay by an active process of exclusion – by the man making of her the boundary of what can be tolerated – clarifies many of the difficulties in sexual relations which reappear in the therapeutic process itself. Women are constructed as literally *marginal to* (on the margins of) rational, masculine discourse; femininity marks the difference between what is symbolisable and what is not; consequently, between what can be controlled and what threatens to explode, engulf or subvert. Moi presents this idea in an exceptionally clear fashion, worth quoting at some length:

Women seen as the limit of the symbolic order will ... share in the disconcerting properties of *all* frontiers: they will be neither inside nor outside, neither known nor unknown. It is this position that has enabled male culture sometimes to vilify women as signifying darkness and chaos, to view them as Lilith or the whore of Babylon, and sometimes to elevate them as the representatives of a higher and purer nature, to venerate them as Virgins and Mothers of God. In the first instance the borderline is seen as part of the chaotic wilderness outside, and in the second it is seen as an inherent part of the inside: the part that protects and shields the symbolic order from imaginary chaos.

(Moi, 1985, p. 167)

The idea of the marginality of 'woman' is actually a method whereby she is placed as an imaginary frontier between rationality and irrationality – indeed, a frontier marking off the Symbolic from what is outside it, the sane from the mad. Sometimes this produces an idealisation: as frontier, she is in direct contact with that which lies outside and can offer salvation; more often, she represents a threat to masculine purity, to balance and control. Whichever tendency dominates, 'woman' here is a product of imagination, literally the Imaginary; a fantasy that holds masculinity in place. Moreover, she is a *spatial* fantasy, a kind of boundary around a safe terrain – a theme, as will be seen below, which recurs when the gender politics of therapy are considered. It is already implicit in the imagery employed by Moi in the quotation above: when in idealised mode, the woman is 'an inherent part of the inside: the part that protects and shields the symbolic order from imaginary chaos'. In other words, she offers a boundary of containment, something protective allowing what is inside to survive. This, too, is amongst the commonest of all images of the therapeutic task.

The masculine strategy is to exclude the feminine, marking the boundaries of his own unstable identity by reifying and repudiating the other. As was argued in the previous chapter, this process leaves its mark on the man: born out of a terror of disappearance in the other, it creates a division based on negativity rather than on the construction of a positive identity and engagement with difference. Benjamin (1988, p. 65) comments that, 'The master's denial of the other's subjectivity leaves him faced with isolation as the only alternative to being engulfed by the dehumanised other'. In this situation, desperate strategies of contact are sometimes employed: 'The underlying theme of sadism is the attempt to break through to the other. The desire to be discovered underlies its counterpart, namely masochism' (*ibid.*, pp. 71–2). Lacan's 'There is no such thing as *The Woman*' is more playful than this, more knowing of its consequences and of the ripples its rhetoric will create. But it is of the same order as all masculine denials of the feminine, all appropriations of the woman's distinct and powerful voice that does not in fact want to be *spoken for*, in any sense of those words. It denies the other so as to create a boundary around what is experienced as an incoherent self; it uses the woman as contrast or limit, but always as something which will make the man feel safe.

There is a delicate dynamic of time and space here that will be explored in the next section. But before moving on it is worth making a further point which is linked with some of the material in the previous chapter. There, it was suggested that the straightforward opposition to all things male proposed by some radical feminists can be a mirror of the masculine repudiation of femininity; somehow undermining the *certainty* of sexual difference in this fixed form is a more promising avenue for progression to a less constricted set of gendered states. Kristeva makes a point consistent with this in the following invocation of the ideal therapeutic stance. Writing about the possible position of the psychoanalyst, she outlines a relatively conventional distinction between masculine and feminine, paternal and maternal, using (admittedly in brackets), a familiar name from British psychoanalysis.

> The analyst situates himself on a ridge where, on the one hand, the 'maternal' position – gratifying needs, 'holding' (Winnicott) – and on the other the 'paternal' position – the differentiation, distance and pro-hibition that produces both meaning and absurdity – are intermingled and severed, infinitely and without end.
>
> (Kristeva, 1983, p. 246)

This vision of a 'ridge', where the conventions of femininity and masculinity meet, interferes with the apparent clarity of the idea of a fixed sexual difference that produces meaning and is causal in the determination of people's consciousness and of all symbolic relationships. Kristeva implies that the analyst ('he') can transcend this difference, can be both feminine and masculine, maternal and paternal; in fact, the instance of maternity offered in the quotation is a (bracketed) man, Winnicott.

One might ask what magic this is, that desexes the analyst? When is a man not a man? The conventional answer is that with the denial of sexual difference we are in the arena of hysteria; does this make all analysts into hysterics? As noted in Chapter 4, Lacan is reputed to have said of himself that he was the perfect hysteric – one without symptoms. He was known as 'the Master', but according to Roudinesco (1986, p. 513), 'With men, the master acted as an abusive mother and with women as a Don Juan or a protective father. With all concerned, he flaunted his femininity.' What the material on woman as fantasised limit of man, as well as this idea about the androgyny of the analyst, suggests is that there is no certainty when it comes to questions of masculine and feminine, subject and object, speaker and spoken of. So when it comes to thinking about the analytic encounter, the space and time in which a patient and a therapist talk to and fantasise about each other, sexual difference should start to become something else – something fluid and subversive, questioning whatever it is that the protagonists might bring.

TIME AND SPACE

In a collection of papers entitled *Between Feminism and Psychoanalysis* (Brennan, 1989), a debate is initiated about the nature of analytic time. One of the contributors, Rosi Braidotti, suggests that an 'ethical aim' of psychoanalysis is to lead the analysand to an acceptance of the 'great master' time. Time here seems to be linked with death and through that to an acceptance of naturalness, of limitation: the passing of generations. According to this view, psychoanalysis is a process that aims to enable the subject to be reconciled with otherness, to acknowledge the power of what lies outside. This involves acknowledging 'the great master' – a gendered word of course, evoking Lacan – who is not the analyst, but time. Despite its Lacanian gloss, this is a message in line with Freud's own impression about the limited nature of psychoanalysis' therapeutic optimism: conversion of 'hysterical misery' into 'common unhappiness', in its most famous, though admittedly early, formulation (Breuer and Freud, 1895, p. 393). Psychoanalysis, in this view of things, can do no more than enable the patient to understand the boundaries of her or his own existence and to comprehend and accept the decline of omnipotent fantasies; that is, it facilitates a more balanced relationship with reality.

Irigaray, in the same collection as Braidotti, makes a comment which relates to this discourse on time, but which is more imbued with sexuality and also with a recognition of the ambiguity of the notion of reality – the way what appears to be necessary (that which must be accepted) might alternatively be seen as constructed and alienated, an aberration rather than a state of nature. She writes:

> Where once there was birth, growth, natural and plant cycles, is now the construction of artificial cultures with strange gods and heavenly bodies, labyrinthine laws and rules, founded in hidden mania, full of terrors, prohibitions, excessive, pathogenic, confused *jouissance*.
>
> (Irigaray, 1989, p. 137)

Irigaray contrasts what is natural with what is artificial; what is natural is cyclical, organic; what is artificial is labyrinthine, subject to the law. If we are not yet in the world of Kafka here, we are close to that of Oedipus: the natural is maternal, the prohibition paternal. Yet, the use of the word *'jouissance'*, with its connotation of an eruptive and subversive kind of sexualised pleasure, maintains an ambiguity which is characteristic of postmodernism. Irigaray refers back to a previous state – an imaginary time when there was 'birth, growth, natural and plant cycles', when human subjectivity was at one with nature. Nowadays, in contrast, there is alienation born from artificiality, but these artificial cultures, while 'confused' and 'pathogenic', do give us *'jouissance'*, the thrill of a pleasure which cannot be contained. Moving away from the natural to the artificial does not lead only to loss. Ironically, too, the end word given to characterise this apparently paternal nexus, *'jouissance'*, is, in Lacan's work at least, usually applied to feminine rather than masculine sexuality. Already in this material there is subversion of what might seem an obvious polarity, between feminine nature and masculine culture; something 'feminine' lives in the latter as well.

The confusion of masculine and feminine positions has already been referred to as part of the discourse of 'hysteria'. As was described in Chapter 2, Freud's encounter with hysteria was in many respects the founding moment of psychoanalysis: facing his patients, their symptoms played out on their bodies, he allowed them to speak, and in so doing made a space for 'the irrational discourse of femininity in the realm of science' (Moi, 1989, p. 196). 'Psychoanalysis', writes Grosz (1990, p. 6), 'is formed out of the "raw material" of women's desire to talk and Freud's desire to listen.' The ambiguity of all this is very obvious, even leaving aside the strong sense in which Freud himself identifies with his hysterical patients, particularly when analysing his own dreams (see Chapter 3). Freud transgresses the boundary between masculine and feminine, subject and object: he allows the hysterical female her voice, her subjectivity, and becomes a receptive object for it. In doing so, he allows for the existence of 'another scene' – perhaps femininity, perhaps the unconscious itself. On the other hand, this man, this clever coloniser of the mind and of the discourse of the hysteric, makes of the newly speaking subject woman another object, a dark continent banged into shape, made 'subject to' the rules and regulations of another's ideas. The interplay in operation here is the common one between power and knowledge: irrationality, identified with the feminine, is allowed its voice so as to be better understood, to be subjected to rational discourse. By naming what is going on, we cease to be ravished by it.

Despite the ambiguity of sexual difference symbolised by hysteria – according to Ragland-Sullivan (1991, pp. 58–9), 'entry into psychoanalysis has the effect of hystericising any patient . . . insofar as talking, questioning, trying to know, produces a search for the missing signifier for Woman' – its most common representation is as an encounter between a female patient and a male analyst, gazing at her and occasionally listening to her voice. Freud's (1905) 'Dora' case study is the classic exemplar of this encounter. This piece was originally written with the conscious intention of offering illustrations of the dream theory in practice, but gradually developed into a source for exploration of a number of key issues in psychoanalysis: transference, countertransference, and feminine sexuality (see Bernheimer and Kahane, 1985, for a collection of important essays on 'Dora'). Here, I want to mention briefly just two related points that concern the rendering of hysteria in 'Dora' and the fixedness or otherwise of sexual difference.

The first concerns the subversiveness of the text itself. It is apparent from Freud's own remarks and from the tone of much of the case history, that Freud's writing is driven partly by a desire to come to terms with the 'fragmented' nature of his analysis of Dora and its uncertain outcome, in which she leaves him before he is ready for her to go. To some extent this is a scholarly and therapeutic activity of working out and working through what happened, but to some extent it is a form of revenge. Freud writes Dora into history, case history and the history of ideas. From his own account (the only one available) of the analysis, he seems to own Dora, knowing her better than she knows herself, positioning her with his mastery, using her 'case' as an example of his own ideas. For everything she brings, he has an answer, and often one which she does not like. She can deny his interpretations, but he knows that he knows best – and in the end, even though she leaves, she seems to submit. Historically, it would appear that she has to: after all, it is Freud's version of things which comes down to us, and he has a great deal of authority.

Yet, the actual history of this text is much more open than might be expected. Presented as an illustrative case history of an hysteric, it has become a number of different things: a source for feminist inspiration, a document of resistance and recovery, a modernist novella, a problematic of Freud and love. As Freud pins Dora down, so she slips away, eventually leaving him, for better or worse. As he writes the story, so it rewrites itself, revealing Freud's own fascinations and inhibitions – for example, famously, when he claims he always speaks openly about sex, but can only reproduce this openness in the text by lapsing into French (1905, p. 82). The apparent objectivity of the work slides into a complex expression of what might be called a three-way unconscious: Dora's, Freud's, and the text's. And now, in contemporary debates, 'Dora' is perhaps the most famous Freudian text of all: open as it is to everyone, most writers on psychoanalysis and sexual difference have had something to say about it, wrestling to produce new meanings that throw light on femininity, masculinity and desire. Freud's mastery has long gone; this textual unconscious, this irrationality, subverts all attempts to conquer it by reason. In this way, 'Dora' demonstrates not only that texts, once written, have lives of their own – which patently they do – but also that when the text is so obviously about sexual difference, all sorts of unexpected pleasures can be found.

The second point concerns the exchange of women in a culture of men. Dora's father brings her to Freud with a request that she should be helped to see reality in the way that *he* sees it – basically, that she should agree to play her part in his affair with Frau K. Freud is both too astute and too honest to work according to another man's agenda, but he does nevertheless find himself caught up in a network of liaisons and identifications from which he cannot easily extricate himself. At its most straightforward, Freud recognises the manner in which Dora is oppressively positioned between two men (her father and Herr K.) working in some kind of collusion with one other, but he also identifies with both of them, particularly Herr K. Moreover, however much Freud creates a setting in which Dora's positive desire might be acknowledged – a space for feminine sexuality – he continues to see her as a term in a masculine economy. In the first edition of the case study, he writes (incorrectly, as he later reports) that she was later married to a putative lover who has appeared as an association to one of her dreams, as if this masculine destination is the obvious one for her. In a long footnote, however, Freud reveals the feminine determinants of Dora's desire – her love for Frau K. Freud is unable to see this clearly, to rid himself of his status as subject and understand how he might be an object in an economy of feminine desire; as Jacobus (1986, p. 42) puts it, he is 'blinkered when it comes to a triangle in which the man mediates between two women, as he himself mediates between Dora and the (m)other woman'. Dora, however, asserts her own positive status and resists Freud to the end, treating him like a servant, giving him two weeks' notice, then going. In this sense, she uses him and remains free of him, as he fails to recognise her desire fully. On the other hand, there is some evidence (see Bernheimer and Kahane, 1985) that she stayed a hysteric all her life. Who 'won' the battle between her and Freud is therefore a debateable point; but something which is clear is that Dora was not simply possessed by him, that she was able in analysis to create some kind of space of her own.

Hysteria, then, cannot be thought of simply as the 'female malady', because it makes questions of sexual difference, identity and power problematic. Its meshing together of body and word removes the clarity of vision so prized by the masculine order. As the man looks in upon it, trying to maintain his distance, so he gets drawn in, becomes one of the characters in a tale he thinks he is writing from outside. Something about the kind of feminine subversiveness that is 'hysteria' is absorbing and tricky, and when it is faced with the equally absorbing and tricky procedures of psychoanalysis, it produces a space in which established and accepted boundaries become unstable and partially dissolved. This may be why hysteria, according to Freud as read by Kristeva, is regarded as a malady of space.

It was suggested earlier that psychoanalysis is in part about recovering an appreciation of time, submitting to its mastery – something which at its most abstract seems to be a masculine association. But if that is so, then the literature reveals there to be quite a tussle going on over the nature and meaning of time. This tussle has the following, complexly interwoven form: one, the feminine is the domain of space, the masculine of time; two, time and space flow into one another, journey without end. Kristeva (1979) writes, 'when evoking the name and destiny of women, one thinks more of the *space* generating and forming the human species than of *time*, becoming or history' (p. 190). Taken at face value, this is a conventional and familiar gendering of things: the feminine, because of the womb and the maternal function, is associated with space, in the sense of both a place from which something is produced, and one in which something is received, enclosed and held. The masculine dimension, however, is active: the male does things, creates history, writes books and speaks words that have an effect. However, no such simple differentiation can be sustained in Kristeva's work. We have already encountered her saying that the analyst can combine maternal and paternal, holding and differentiation, in a sense combining these stereotypic illuminations of space and time. Now Kristeva complicates any easy identity of masculinity with time and femininity with space – having versus holding – by arguing that it is not that women *are* space rather than time, but that their time is like space; it has space-like qualities.

In 'Women's Time' (1979, p. 191), Kristeva claims that, from amongst the 'multiple modalities of time known through the history of civilisations', female subjectivity essentially retains two forms: 'repetition' and 'eternity'. The former is seen in those aspects of femininity which have a cyclical and rhythmic quality and hence a relationship with nature which is both regular and exhilarating – both pleasurable in its stereotyped patterning and subversive in its link with 'what is experienced as extra-subjective time, cosmic time'. Women's time as 'eternity' takes a somewhat different form: 'the massive presence of a monumental temporality, without cleavage or escape' – something sombre, unscalable, immoveable in its solidity, something always present.

Thus, women's time is not men's time, but it is time nevertheless. It is rather like Irigaray's 'natural cycles', but it seems more frightening than that: it is hysterical time in that it is akin to the movements of the body, 'cyclical or monumental'. It opposes masculine time, named by Kristeva as 'time as project, teleology, linear and prospective unfolding; time as departure, progression and arrival – in other words, the time of history' (1979, p. 192). This masculine time sounds like narrative time, story time; Kristeva writes that 'A psychoanalyst would call this "obsessional time", recognising in the mastery of time the true structure of the slave' (*ibid.*). Ironically, Lacan was expelled from the psychoanalytic movement on the grounds of his fiddling around with the boundaries of time – varying the length of sessions according to his patients' needs, or his own. Indeed, with all the emphasis psychoanalysts place on creating a therapeutic space, it is the very fixed boundaries of a certain time limit (usually fifty minutes) that offer the strongest definition of what that space is about.

Of course, none of this is straightforward. Kristeva claims that feminine time is both cyclical and monumental. It is, therefore, akin to analytic time: time that carves out a space. There is no beginning or end, therapy is not about doing but about staying – in the Kleinian vision, for instance, it is about the capacity of the analyst to remain a constant and surviving figure in the face of the projected onslaughts of the patient's destructive emotions or aspects of self. In this respect, there is a significant, gendered dimension to the Kleinian development: where Freudian analysis is characterised by an orientation towards reconstruction of the narratives of the past, and hence emphasises the cognitive and developmental dimensions of insight, Kleinian analysis is immersed in an ever-unfolding present, where the here-and-now interchange of highly charged emotions is of primary concern. Masculine time, masculine therapy, is the time of doing, of first and second and last; feminine time and therapy is that of being, of waxing, waning and waxing again, of holding.

But therapy is not simply masculine or feminine in this sense, not *either* revealing the history of a complaint *or* exploring the emotional context in which symptoms currently exist. Therapy is a space, but not just a safe haven; it is a *generative* space in which a struggle occurs for the production of new meanings – as in 'Dora', a stream of signifiers producing difference. Therapy therefore encompasses both masculine time and feminine time, but how, and in what form, and to what degree may depend on the dimensions of difference present in the room. Are we talking here of a feminine space punctuated by masculine insertions; or of a struggle for mastery held in bounds by the caress of a containing temporal structure; or perhaps of an hysterical dissolution of 'masculinity' and 'femininity' into an imaginary bisexuality? Or, perhaps, we are back with the imagery of giving birth: a space that, over time, produces something new. Here, as ever, as in the discussion of the seeds of masculine sexuality, as in Kristeva's reading of Winnicott, we are in the realm of the mother.

SPEAKING WITH THE MOTHER

Irigaray is once again relevant here. 'Woman always speaks *with* the mother; man speaks in her absence' (1989, p. 134). However, this 'speaking with' is not necessarily to be construed as something positive, as a mode of care and containment – the idealised version of Winnicott and even, in some readings, of Klein. For Irigaray, maternal space, in the absence of a symbolic account of the mother which is not constructed from the masculine position – that is, which is not constructed from within the Lacanian Symbolic – is an untheorisable space always threatening to turn into engulfment. Her focus is on the significance of the early, pre-Oedipal mother–daughter relationship, but her argument is that this cannot be symbolised properly under patriarchy, given the way the phallic nature of the Symbolic order intervenes. That is, the mediation of all symbolic activity by the lens of phallic discourse wipes out the mother as woman, contributing to misogyny but also, more importantly here, distorting the account of the pre-Oedipal Imaginary so that it becomes impossible to discover the meaning of the feminine in its own terms. As Wright (1989) points out, this is true of psychoanalysis itself, which tends to examine the mother in terms of *whose property* she is – whether the child or the father, but not in terms of her own positive content. Irigaray herself points out that this lack of a language of the feminine, lack of a true symbolic of difference, leaves the daughter and her mother always absorbed within each other.

> The mother always remains too familiar and too close. The girl has the mother, in some sense, in her skin, in the humidity of the mucous membranes, in the intimacy of her most intimate parts, in the mystery of her relation to gestation, birth, and to her sexual identity.
>
> (Irigaray, 1989, p. 133)

Speaking 'with' the mother means not being able to represent the mother–daughter relationship in terms of both intensity (which is genuine) and difference (which is potential). So the masculine difficulty in separating from the mother while remaining in contact with her is matched by the feminine difficulty of becoming a subject at all.

According to Whitford, Irigaray reads women's ontological status in this culture as 'déréliction', 'the state of abandonment, described significantly in the same terms (un *fusionnel*) as the psychoanalytic term for women's failure to individuate and differentiate themselves from their mother' (Whitford, 1989, p. 112). By contrast, men have a kind of space which is truly their own: 'the fundamental ontological category for men is *habiter* (dwelling), whether in a literal or a figurative sense: men live in "grottoes, huts, women, towns, language, concepts, theories, etc." ' (*ibid.*). So here it is men who have a room of their own; the woman's space turns into absorption in the mother – once again, in a way, she ceases to exist. But there is something else as well, a way in which this non-existence can make itself felt. Grosz, building on Irigaray's work and emphasising the way phallocentric discourse has made the woman's voice unattainable, draws out the consequences of this non-existence in terms which suggest both its pathology and its potential for subversion.

> As the sexual other to the One sex, woman has only been able to speak or to be heard as an undertone, a murmur, a rupture within discourse; or else she finds her expression in a hysterical fury, where the body 'speaks' a discourse that cannot be verbalised by her.
>
> (Grosz, 1990, p. 174)

This idea of an undertone, a murmur, will be returned to later in connection with Kristeva's notion of the semiotic; it suggests something alluring and threatening, something holding the possibility of overturning the dominant order of things.

For the moment, however, let us ask the question of what kind of space it is that men inhabit and offer, what might be the nature of this speaking in the absence of the mother that is also a kind of possession, a dwelling in the woman as well as in the Symbolic. Certainly, men work in culture: rationality rules, but – as was discussed in the previous chapter – at a substantial price, that of disowning most of what exists. One possible critical route here would be to take up the work of Cixous, to emphasise the subversiveness of the feminine disruption of all forms of continuity, to elaborate the rhythmic and the emotional, to speak the *'jouissance'* of the unconscious. All these are meant to be characteristic 'feminine' modes of activity, not necessarily excluding individual men, but built on the premise of a relationship with the body from which most men are very distant. Then this stable place of the man, this 'habiter', ceases to look so promising, and the dereliction of femininity is no longer a state of absence. This also would have the effect of revalorising Irigaray's reading of feminine sexuality as plural – always at least two, not pinned down to the monolithic and imaginary masculine unity. Indeed, Irigaray's general point concerning multiplicity is important here, and presents a vision which is shared by many feminist writers. This is that the monolithic nature of the masculine sexual economy, symbolised by the penis = phallus equation, is one built on a reasoning process in which polarities are constructed (either/or) and then one pole is repudiated (male/female). Gallop (1988, p. 97) comments, 'Irigaray seems to be advocating a female sexuality that replaces the anxious either–or with a pleasurable both: vagina and clitoris'. Why should there be only one thing at a time, and why should that thing always be male?

As Gallop (1988) points out, the destabilising process set in motion by the prospect of non-phallic modes of sexual identity has a critical impact on the Lacanian assertion of the primacy of the phallus and of its distinction from the penis. The importance of this claimed distinction ('the phallus is not the penis') is that it cuts across genderedness to make both female and male castrated in language – neither is the source of power, the true originator of meaning. Yet, as Gallop emphasises and as was discussed in Chapter 5, the phallus is not in fact some totally arbitrary symbol, it is built up on the model of the penis, and it is masculinity which is associated both with the phallus and with power. As we have seen, Lacan himself, in 'The Meaning of the Phallus' and elsewhere, is unable to counter this identity persuasively, limiting his positive rendering of the nature of the phallus to the slogan that 'the phallus can only play its role as veiled' (Lacan, 1958, p. 82). Veils usually connote the feminine, but try as Lacan might to desex the organ, the phallus/penis relationship does seem stubbornly resistant to denial.

In her inimitable style, Gallop forces her way through all this:

> The Lacanians' desire clearly to separate *phallus* from *penis*, to control the meaning of the signifier *phallus*, is precisely symptomatic of their desire to have the phallus, that is, their desire to be at the centre of language, at its origin. And their inability to control the meaning of the word *phallus* is evidence of what Lacan calls symbolic castration.
>
> (Gallop, 1988, p. 126)

The Lacanians are here hoist with their own petard, revealing their desire, but unable to enforce it because of the slipperiness of desire itself. In an important sense, this failure represents a rupture in the Symbolic order; that which appears to be in control is actually at a loss when faced with the positive challenge of language, the unconscious, and femininity. In this way, femininity breaks through with the beginnings of its own Imaginary; the possibility is raised of an alternative frame of reference and way of thinking about the relationship of sexual difference to the phallus – that is, to 'power, language and meaning'.

This brings this discussion back to Kristeva. Kristeva is not willing to dispense with the idea of the Symbolic; on the contrary, she argues that sexual difference will only ever become intelligible through the development of theory concerning this order of representation. However, what Kristeva does – in a move which is as much as anything her most substantial contribution to feminist psychoanalytic thinking – is to re-examine the relationship between pre-Oedipal and Oedipal registers, or rather, between the Imaginary and the Symbolic, to produce an account of their interweaving which is more subtle than that offered by Lacan, and which leaves open many more possibilities for movement and development. Simply put, this re-examination involves the revising of the Imaginary as an order of 'semiotic' functioning, which (as with the Imaginary) is surpassed when the Symbolic comes into being, but which is also a necessary and continuing pre-condition of the Symbolic – and a source of opposition to, and disruption of, symbolic functioning.

Grosz offers one of the clearest available descriptions of the notion of the semiotic, and its relationship with the Symbolic, as follows:

> The semiotic is a set of pre-signifying impulses and drives that chaotically circulate in and through the infant's body; the Symbolic consists in the replacement of these polymorphous body impulses and libidinal drives through their hierarchical subsumption in the Oedipus Complex, through which these impulses are harnessed in social production ... The semiotic (mythically, retroactively) precedes and exceeds the Symbolic, overflowing and problematising its boundaries. In the broadest terms, the semiotic is the input of the undirected body, while the Symbolic is the regulated use and organised operations of that body in social production. It is only through the Symbolic that we can have access to the semiotic; the former provides the latter with a voice and a mode of representation.
>
> (Grosz, 1992, p. 195)

It will be apparent from this that the semiotic is more easily regarded as a register for femininity – bodily, chaotic, made marginal by the operations of the Symbolic order, unable to speak its own name. In addition, in a simple developmental sense its location as pre-Oedipal makes it, within the conventions of psychoanalysis, something concerned primarily with the mother and hence with the sphere of femininity. But there are some important qualifying points to make here.

The first is that, while acknowledging the shared marginality of the semiotic and the feminine, Kristeva is categorical in maintaining the Freudian and Lacanian assertion that sexual difference is an Oedipal acquisition, making itself felt retrospectively once the castration complex has been enacted, but not actually operating in the pre-Oedipal period itself. Thus, although many writers, particularly feminists, emphasise the genuinely feminine associations of the semiotic (e.g. 'the symbolic/oedipal/social mode owes a debt of existence to an unspeakable and unrepresentable semiotic/maternal/feminine . . . This debt is the social equivalent of the debt the subject owes to a female corporeality which remains unrecognised in its autonomy . . . Kristeva considers the semiotic as a feminine and maternally structured space . . . It is a pre-patriarchal phase in which the *phallic* mother is pre-eminent' [Grosz, 1990, pp. 153, 160]); and although it is also true that in Kristeva's account the semiotic is founded on the primeval space of what she calls the maternal 'chora', emphasising its bodily, enveloping and female quality; nevertheless, her insistence on its pre-gendered nature makes it a possible site of resistance and subversion in all subjective experience – male as well as female. Moi (1985, p. 165) states the position simply as follows: 'Any strengthening of the semiotic, which knows no sexual difference, must therefore lead to a weakening of traditional gender divisions, and not at all to a reinforcement of traditional notions of "femininity" '. *All* subjects are infiltrated by both the Symbolic and the semiotic, subjected to the law but also 'ruptured by the boundless play of semiotic drives' (Elliott, 1992, p. 222). As long as the semiotic exists – which will be always, for the Symbolic would have no materials out of which to be constructed, were it not for the bodily drives rhythmically expressed in the semiotic register – there is a prospect for heterogeneity and disruption within every subject, male or female, and this prospect can always be glimpsed somewhere, whether in art, in language, in madness or in dreams.

In developing this argument, Kristeva retains a vision of what masculinity might contribute to the developmental and social process. Perhaps showing her indebtedness to Klein (a presence rife in 'Freud and Love', as Jacobus [1990] shows), this contribution appears in a kind of pre-Oedipal triangulation, in which the father has a position even prior to his appearance as representative of the law. But whereas Klein incorporates this potentially outside other *within* the relationship with the mother – for instance making the paternal penis part of the phantasy of the maternal breast – Kristeva strives to renounce the narcissism involved in this kind of fusion. Lacanians might say, if forced to be categorical, that the first desire is to be the desire of the mother; Kristeva's point is that even that desire is already directed outside the self–other circuit, towards a separate space. For Kristeva (1983), thinking about Freud and love (and perhaps of her love for Freud), this space is that of the 'father of individual prehistory'.

We plunge, here, into transference – and not just that belonging to Kristeva. Absorbed in the discourse of the patient, the analyst discovers something else, some other speaking presence, some other point towards which the narrative is moving, or, rather, against which it is making itself heard. In Lacan's rendering of this experience, it is patently Oedipal: it is not the immediate relationship with the other but instead the 'big Other' which is at the heart of meaning. That is, there is some outside element, usually theorised as the cultural Law or the imperatives of language, that 'guarantees' meaning by structuring the possibility of all other relationships, whether they take the form of 'analysis or love' (Forrester, 1987, p. 71). Thus, not just the one-person relationship, of self to itself, but also the two-person relationship, of self to other and of infant to mother, is an intrinsically narcissistic one if left unmediated by a third party – the big Other or structures of the Symbolic Law. The target of psychoanalysis is to bring the patient into contact with this outside voice, to show how it operates on her or his own history.

In large part, it is transference that promotes this process. Transference experiences, at least when they are interpreted, move the subject away from her or his narcissism towards an insertion into the Symbolic, into the discourse of the Other. In this respect, Kristeva takes up a very radical position. One effect of the Lacanian structure is to make problematic the refusal of mastery which is supposed to be at the heart of Lacanian theory – a contradiction which is perhaps inextricably linked to the masculine orientation of the theory and to the speciousness of much of its apparent flirtation with femininity. In calling upon the big Other of the Law a certain amount of fetishising of the Symbolic takes place and a phallic theory is created – the notion that, in therapy, we are positioned by reference to something outside us slides easily into an attempt to uncover and identify that something, to unveil the phallus. Kristeva insists that this is too static a position, that the transference relation must be kept dynamic and metaphoric, understood as 'the crystallisation of fantasy' (1983, p. 247) but nevertheless also as something in motion, a 'movement towards the discernible, a journey towards the visible' (ibid.). With everything always in motion, phallic turgidity – full knowledge and mastery in the trans-ference, for example – gives way to that fluidity in terms of which femininity always couches its challenge, and in terms of which the semiotic order is conceived. Psychoanalysts working in a range of different schools of thought have suggested the importance of primary narcissism for the construction of a stable and secure personality (see Frosh, 1991). This is challenged by Lacanians, for whom primary narcissism is itself set up on the model of a fantasised relationship with an imaginary object – the reflection in the mirror. For Kristeva, it is more subtle still. Primary narcissism is structured as a 'parry', as a means of escaping emptiness and the horror of dissolution. 'Narcissism protects emptiness, causes it to exist, and thus, as lining of that emptiness, ensures an elementary separation' (1983, p. 242). The 'abject' is the term applied by Kristeva to this elementary, pre-subjective separation; abject because it is marked by horror, because the subject, constituted as an experiential emptiness, always tends towards falling into a space of nothingness. 'If the object secures the subject in a more or less stable position,' comments Grosz (1992, p. 198), 'the abject signals the fading or disappearance, the absolute mortality and vulnerability of the subject's relation to and dependence on the object.' The fragility of this early subject/object boundary is extreme, making this first motion of the subject-to-be one that can be overwhelmed, producing a state of genuine abjection, of being devoured – of what might be described as 'borderline'. Without mediation, this is precisely what happens in the relationship between the desiring mother and the despairing infant; that is, if the mother's desire is turned towards the child, there is no possibility of a truly maternal 'space', for space disappears and boundaries dissolve.

Here, partly parenthetically, is an element in Kristeva's critique of Klein, and a moment to reintroduce the space created by the father. Taking up the Kleinian assumption that the mother incorporates all the phallic elements of the father, making them her own, Kristeva argues that, while the pre-Oedipal mother is certainly phallic in the sense of being the focus of all the infant's desire, there is something outside her from the start, something towards which the mother can look, preventing her from falling into total absorption in, and identification with, her child. For Kristeva, this 'something' is termed the 'father of individual prehistory', or, as a riposte to Klein, the 'archaic inscription of the father'. Kristeva states, 'The archaic inscription of the father seems to me a way of modifying the fantasy of a phallic mother playing at the phallus game all by herself, alone and complete, in the back room of Kleinianism and post-Kleinianism' (1983, p. 259).

The father of individual prehistory is presented by Kristeva as an entity in the Imaginary sphere – as something therefore clearly operating differently from, but also in conjunction with, the Symbolic father of the Lacanian Law. Kristeva conjures up the archaic father in the pre-Oedipal context of the mother, and specifically as an object towards whom the mother can look, turning her desire away from the infant, and so creating a space into which that infant can grow. Kristeva writes that:

The loving mother, different from the caring and clinging mother, is someone who has an object of desire; beyond that, she has an Other in relation to whom the child will serve as a go-between ... Without the maternal 'diversion' towards a Third Party, the bodily exchange is abjection or devouring.

(Kristeva, 1983, p. 251)

In Lacanian thought, the mother is always partly structured by the law of the father, as an entity both in and at the boundaries of the Symbolic. But here, Kristeva is working with an idea of the mother as *subject* in a different sense – as having something which is her own (a desire for another) that offers her a space which is also her own (she is not defined solely in terms of her mothering function) and that also makes it possible for the infant to resist being submerged in her closeness and immediacy. This is a theoretical move that opens onto a much more fluid field of gender possibilities than that made available in traditional psychoanalytic thinking. In relation to the father, Kristeva opposes the Lacanian implication of a fixed Symbolic order defined by the phallus and by the paternal 'No' (fatherhood as a prohibiting function). Instead, she argues for the importance of a more heterogeneous experience of the father – both in the Imaginary and in the Symbolic, something that both creates a supportive space and that makes symbolic regulation and expression possible.

Here, for example, is her argument concerning the way the use of symbols (a talking cure, perhaps) promotes the 'triumph over sadness' necessary for recovery from depression. What makes this possible, she writes, is the ability of the individual to identify with something other than the lost object – a traditionally Oedipal scenario. However, this outside figure or 'Third Party' is enabling rather than prohibitive, preventing the subject from being engulfed by the lost object. As such, the third party is the 'imaginary father' who functions in exactly this way – creating a space for the infant's subjectivity – in earliest development. Nevertheless, writes Kristeva:

> it is imperative that this father in individual prehistory be capable of playing his part as oedipal father in symbolic Law, for it is on the basis of that harmonious blending of the two facets of fatherhood that the abstract and arbitrary signs of communication may be fortunate enough to be tied to the affective meaning of prehistorical identifications, and the dead language of the potentially depressive person can arrive at a live meaning in the bond with others.

(Kristeva, 1987, pp. 23–4)

As Grosz (1992) points out, this is an image of the imaginary father as something embodying love – contributing to the ambivalence with which many feminists regard Kristeva, as it seems to suggest that the father is superior to the mother in this respect, and more generally that subjectivity can only be secured with the assistance of a patriarchal structure protecting the child against maternal engulfment. However, Kristeva's approach here can equally be seen as a plea for a reinstatement of a different notion of fathering from that defined solely by domination – and she specifically notes that it is only in the combination of the imaginary father with the Oedipal one that symbolic activity can become truly alive.

This is what, ideally anyway, is experienced in the transference during psychoanalysis, and is hinted at in the notion from Kristeva, quoted earlier, that the analyst can hold both 'maternal' and 'paternal' positions. But there is something more at work here, both therapeutically and developmentally, that expresses the openness of the possibilities created by Kristeva's work. If, as in Lacanian theory, the 'Third Party' representing the father and the outside world operates only in the Symbolic as a structure of law and prohibition determining signification, then desire has a kind of closure around it. However much it is constituted in and by lack, it always has its answer in the phallus – something distinct to which it is directed. As has been argued above and in Chapter 5, Lacan's strategy of calling the phallus 'veiled', so making it a slippery and ultimately undefinable entity, does not fully protect it from becoming caught up in the gendered realities of the penis and male power. For Kristeva, however, despite her own argument that the father is always a phallic figure, the imaginary father of individual prehistory is not defined so much by a process of turning *towards* something as of the mother turning *away*, establishing both her own entitlement and that of the infant. Consequently, the nature of the original third party, by being denied Oedipalisation, is left literally questionable.

> The most archaic unity that we thus retrieve . . . is that of the phallus desired by the mother. It is the unity of the imaginary father, a coagulation of the other and her desire. The imaginary father would thus be an indication that the mother is not complete but that she wants . . . Who? What? The question has no answer other than the one that uncovers narcissistic emptiness: 'At any rate, not I'.
>
> (Kristeva, 1983, pp. 256–7)

The direction of the mother's desire away from the infant makes it possible to create a maternal space; in that way, the emptiness of the subject-to-be can become filled, or at least 'blocked up', and turned into 'a producer of signs, representations and meanings' (Kristeva, 1983, p. 258). The presence of, and identification with, this third party, this 'father of individual prehistory', makes all the later history of the subject possible. But this is not a matter of uncovering a real Other – a real father or masculine position, as phallocentric theory and practice might suggest. The gesture that saves the infant subject is the mother's desire being turned away from it (from her or him), the realisation that this desire is for something other than the 'I', something 'not-I' – but what that is is an unanswerable question. The restlessness of desire is what matters most; the certainty, indeed, that, being desire, it has no resting place. So the position of the third party, the 'father', is not that of some distinctly and necessarily gendered positivity, despite its association with both ideal love and Symbolic Law. It is, rather, the creation of a space outside into which the subject can look – making it possible both to be with the mother and to develop. In the process, this involves an enormous range of nurturing and symbolic activities, from the most complex manifestations of subversive semiotic irruptions into oppressive discourse, to the most ordinary question one might ask during a therapeutic transaction: 'What is it that you want?'

'THEIR "SYMBOLIC" EXISTS'

Reading Kristeva as a movement away from Lacan, what is most impressive is the fluidity of the symbolic processes which she uncovers. These build on the genderedness of space and time, and of psychoanalytic practice, but they also produce an idea of how this genderedness can be surpassed – of how the Imaginary dimension of experience can both disrupt and elaborate what is given by the Symbolic. There is no symbolic activity without semiotic processes; moreover, that which appears to be the defining characteristic of the Symbolic – the presence of the paternal third party – can be found in a different form in the most archaic moment of development, when the infant subject first breathes in the prospect of separate being. All of this makes the Symbolic appear much more amenable both to subversion and to enlargement.

Applied to the process of therapy, this work suggests that therapeutic scrutiny should produce an awareness not so much of the maternal container as of the production of a certain kind of other-directedness necessary for survival. None of this is meant to imply that the patriarchal organisation of the contemporary cultural Symbolic is easily overcome: even a cursory look around at the extent of continuing male domination, as well as of the limitations of masculinity, is proof of the difficulty of that process. 'Their "Symbolic" exists,' notes Cixous (1976, p. 255), in a rather different context that asserts the continuing opposition of masculine and feminine, 'it holds power – we, the sowers of disorder, know it only too well'. Recognition of the material reality of this is a necessary pre-condition for activity. In therapeutic terms, it also confirms that the provision of 'maternal space' – 'holding' space – is an important procedure in its own right, making it possible for external power to be bracketed out while exploration of the patient's internal possibilities is undertaken. But what is being argued here is that this morbid opposition – maternal containment, paternal power – is unnecessarily restrictive, however often it is replayed in everyday life. There is always also some other space, a desire that moves outside the mother–infant, therapist–patient orbit. Without this movement, all space collapses – there is no difference. So the conventional distinctions and oppositions – feminine space, masculine time, holding versus doing, repetition versus narrative, hysteria versus obsessionality – these distinctions get taken up into something else, some other intersection of masculinity with femininity, of the Symbolic with the semiotic 'sowers of disorder'.

Narcissism is self-protective, it creates a space for growth; but it can only exist when already premised on structures given from outside. So too with this feminine and this masculine, this 'Ladies and Gentlemen' in Lacan's famous imagery: they protect us, these categories, against the dizzying ambiguities of the fluid unconscious. Neither category, however, is truly 'outside' or other, neither is the 'One' that creates an empathy or a substantive difference. Each is built in relation to the other; perhaps, like space and time, they are 'really' the same thing. As they intersect, and particularly as what is more formal and rational becomes interrupted by what is more disruptive and irrational, some space for imagination and change can be made.

Those woman's tears, with which this chapter began, thus do something more than just state frustration and loneliness or appeal for sensitivity and support. They take up the well-formed narrative of the husband, the domination of his organised story of his life, and make a statement about what else might be going on, what otherness might be in existence – in the therapeutic situation and in their life together. Her tears, her half-silenced sentence and half-articulated silence, draw attention to the oppressive structure within which symbolisation is taking place, and then undermine this to make it impossible for it to continue. By letting the unconscious rhythm of the therapeutic and marital dance break through the constraints of the husband's formal discourse, not only is narrative time stopped, but a new space is created in which it is possible to reflect on the conditions which are holding everything – oppression and power, female and male roles, therapy and collusion, silence and speech – in place.

TRANSGRESSING SEXUAL DIFFERENCE

What impact can this material have, all these words? Let me start from the inside, and move out, to explore whether the power reflected in the statement 'Their "Symbolic" exists' can be averted or overcome as easily as I have suggested above. 'There is always some other space', I claim, building on a particular theoretical reading of Kristeva's work; but can this other space be made manifest, or must it remain utopian, a glimpse of flesh with no prospect of possession?

As the woman cries, breaking into the silence of my response to the man's narrative, it brings home to me the extent to which men's failure to challenge and disrupt one another in our dealings with women always has a collusive quality. This is a very complicated issue in therapy, because the dimension of sexual difference interferes with any straightforward rendering of the relationship between speech and analytic silence. Silence is the traditional mode of disruption employed in the psychoanalytic process. Any well-formed, egoic narrative consciously structured and directed by the patient is distrusted by the analyst; the analyst's response to it is to remain still and let it run its course, listening out for the anxiety which underlies it. In the context of an instruction (the Freudian 'basic rule') just to talk about whatever is in one's mind – an instruction designed to produce fragments and associations rather than wholes – it is anxiety that makes such organised speech necessary, and the therapeutic task is to lay hold of this anxiety and bring it to light. Silence is a means of achieving this end, because it frustrates the expectation of the patient that there will be a response to the content of her or his speech, so breaking apart any prospect of cosy dialogue. This then allows the underpinnings of the patient's speech to be explored, revealing the gap between the composed surface of narrative discourse and the inner experience of splitting and uncertainty. It is at this point that a response – an interpretation, perhaps – is called for: as the patient discovers that her or his formal self-presentation leads nowhere, the analyst can detect a space in which the unconscious can be heard.

For a male therapist, at least, this is how the analytic silence looks from within the Symbolic: the male patient speaks, the expected confirmation from the other man, the therapist, fails to arrive, and this calls into question all received wisdom and all assumptions about what is consensual and what needs to be unpacked. Listening to the man, thinking about what he has to say but not responding, not registering agreement or disagreement, can from within the terms of the Symbolic be a disruptive act. Especially when talking about women, men expect other men to agree – to come up with equally disparaging stories or jokes, perhaps, or to sympathise. The unconscious impulse to do so is enormously powerful, as the misogyny of many apparently progressive men testifies. Consequently, refraining from providing such confirmation can seem an enormously brave step to take, like taking sides against one's own team, calling into question masculine unity. But from outside the masculine order (the woman writes 'Their Symbolic', after all), it can look different, like one man speaking and the other listening uncritically to what he has to say, not taking up the obvious holes in the narrative – for instance and most importantly, not asking what has happened to the woman. Mr A. and I are part of this Symbolic in the simplest sense: we take it for granted that a language between men exists and can exclude women. When the woman cries, it makes me feel that my supposedly disruptive silence in the face of the pressure to confirm the solidarity of men is an act that still resides in the ('Their') Symbolic, having no impact on the isolation which she feels.

My silence in the face of the woman's distress has a different significance from my silent response to the man's story. It is not even remotely disruptive, but rather confirms the existence of the wilderness between us: I am disturbed by her tears, but cannot cross over to reach her. What I recognise in this, what is so subversive about the woman's unconscious position here, is that the whole economy of masculine sameness is being called into question. The observable gradations of progressiveness or misogyny are of importance – that is, it matters how individual men act towards women, how we speak and think, whether we strive to understand and be understood, whether we make a space for difference. Not all manifestations of masculinity are equally oppressive: there is a difference between 'the rapist' and the therapist, even though therapeutic power always includes a possibility of abuse. But what I become aware of, as I try to deconstruct 'masculinity' as a therapist or as a writer, is how this activity can so easily take place only within the masculine dimension – 'Their Symbolic' – without really transgressing any boundaries or making it across the wilderness at all. Whether we speak or not, whether we listen empathically or bark out orders, whether we talk *about* women or ignore them completely, makes no absolute difference in itself. Women watch us at work, an alien spectacle; they are still, in this masculine Symbolic, an object and an other. 'Nobody would be interested', they might all say, 'we know it only too well.'

My pessimism here is part personal disappointment. However hard I might try, or believe I try, it is difficult not to be implicated in the Symbolic, and my own imaginative capacities seem too limited in comparison with the power of that whole order. My uncertainty about the 'masculine' position, described in Chapter 1, does not mean that I am free from the tendency to enjoy phallic mastery, nor from a wish to see femininity enclosed and written off as a narcissistic dimension, so that men – or at least I – might have something specific and different to offer. More to the point, I have now almost completed writing a book on sexual difference, yet still cannot find any words for transgressing gender categories which are not themselves full to overflowing with those categories, which are not, once again, firmly rooted in the masculine ('My') Symbolic. 'Masculine' and 'feminine': these unresolvable terms are still there – both as constructed, empty notions, and as deeply rooted experiences of personal identity.

Is this just a failure of my own imagination or a general difficulty with the construction of a new Imaginary and consequently of an alternative Symbolic? Kristeva's work is exciting because of the implication of semiotic processes in the heart of the Symbolic – because the body never leaves the word alone. Rhythm, energy, style; disintegration, fragment-ation; playfulness, poetry. Whereas Lacan's version of this produces nihilism, Kristeva seems to offer the prospect of recovery of something more complete – both maternal and paternal, in conventional terms.

Everyone can be a subject, it seems; we just all need a certain kind of space in which to begin to live our experience. I want very much to believe in this, to find an end to this book in which all these strands of being can be brought together to represent a range of gender possibilities – something flexible and exciting, therapeutically powerful and socially subversive. However, as the existence of feminist criticism of Kristeva testifies, every time some such an inclusive, integrating tendency comes to the fore, it looks suspiciously like another organised narrative, something else located solely within the terms of the Symbolic itself.

I have argued throughout this book that the tension between deconstructing sexual difference and using gender categories as if they were absolutes is characteristic of psychoanalysis and is one source of its creative power. This is linked with the fluctuation between optimism and pessimism over progress: as traditional gender determination shows its limitations and new possibilities are articulated, so the deep-rootedness of gender identity and the difficulty of overcoming it become apparent. As each of us dreams, like Freud, in both 'feminine' and 'masculine' modes, we encounter premonitions of gender transgression; but perhaps because of the anxiety which that awareness produces, we run back into our received positions, our gendered identities. Lacan punctures the myths of phallic mastery, yet exploits language and his audience in an utterly masterful way: whether he is being ironic or megalomaniac is never clear – perhaps he is both at once. Men wish for the mother and idealise her, but turn this into denigration and violence directed against women and children in a flight from dependency produced by the need for, yet fear of, intimate connection with others. In this chapter, too, there has been described the vision of a new Imaginary which can incorporate an integration of the different aspects of fathering, so reducing the objectification of the woman into 'mother'. But alongside it runs a repudiation of the possibility of change, a suggestion that while there is only a masculine Symbolic, nothing can be shifted.

Inside and out, therefore, it is hard to maintain an optimistic stance towards gender transgression. Everything seems so fixed that with every theoretical step forward there is a practical step back. Indeed, at times one wonders if the use of complex theories of the kind described in this book is precisely an escape from practice – from the real constraints upon action in the world. If we cannot live our gender relations differently, at least we can talk about them in an exciting and seductive way. Especially in an intellectual climate in which 'discourse' is valorised as the prime force in the construction of experience, *talking* differently can come to seem sufficient in its own right. But while this talking continues to take place within the orbit of one master discourse – that of the Symbolic – it can be argued that nothing is really being challenged, that the conversation remains the same.

So where, if anywhere, can the seeds of hope be found? If it is the case that masculinity and femininity are constructed positions, and that sexual difference is something which is built rather than given, then alternative constructions must be available, at least in principle. It is here that the idea of a new Imaginary has most importance, not just as a theoretical conception, but as a bridge to specific practices that can challenge the way in which the Symbolic itself is organised. Even in Lacan's version of things, there is some intersection between the Imaginary and the Symbolic; for Kristeva, it will be recalled, this intersection is a deeply intimate one, in which semiotic fluidity and Symbolic order are mutually interdependent. Imagination, therefore, is a potentially practical activity, revolving alternative visions of experience, other ways of relating to the 'as if' reality of the world. It is also specific rather than general: what may make the difference to sexual difference is the clash between particular instances of the 'sowers of disorder' with the given reality of the Symbolic – cumulative and repetitive, drip-dripping on the rock face until it begins to be worn away. One thing to learn from postmodernism (Lyotard, 1979) is the way 'grand narratives' have given way before the 'little narratives' of coercion and of emancipation; each story told makes a contribution to supporting the Symbolic or to its fading away.

For myself, the encounters documented in this book have some disordering power within them. Thinking to try to come to terms with sexual difference – a grand design, for sure – I have had to deal with a series of specific problems, some as precise as one woman's tears in a session of therapy, others more abstract, but still personalised. It has been just as difficult as I imagined it would be, and just as troublesome a responsibility, but the little narratives keep provoking me with their questions. Both to claim and to repudiate an identity as a man seem impossible positions to hold onto, yet both these positions have to be asserted and the tension between them put to use. Sexual difference itself is something one has somehow to be involved in; it cannot be dismissed or avoided. Each time it is challenged, however, the terms of engagement change and some new dent is made in the assumption that what currently exists in gender relations has always to remain the same. I end this book pessimistic, but not without hope.

My own 'Imaginary', then, runs something like this. 'Masculinity' no longer exists as a category of the subject which can be taken for granted. The content with which it has conventionally been credited – rationality, mastery and the like – is neither a specific attribute of the masculine position nor a sufficient condition for dealing with the conditions of social and psychological existence. With the demise of this category, and partly causing it, the 'feminine' also disappears. Instead, what has usually been given as femininity – from irrationality to *'jouissance'* – exists continually at the margins of personal experience, prodding away eventually to puncture all assertions of full mastery, knowledge and control. What we are left with, much in the spirit of the 'little narratives' of the postmodern condition, is a series of *provisional* positions. Nothing remains settled; as each statement of sexual difference is made, so some other tale gets told. At the same moment in which Freud positions himself as masculine conqueror of the feminine unconscious, he also produces identifications with femininity and opens up his own uncertain desire. As Lacan displays his virility, so he also masquerades in women's clothes, obscuring the phallus with a veil. As I try to think about what it means to be a male therapist, I come face to face with the critical marginality of feminine rejection of the male order as a whole.

It is in what is provisional that the possibility of a more creative future resides – what is not settled and definite, already-known and absolutely under control. That is why the future tense is utopian and revolutionary, and why the unconscious is so disturbing and alluring at once. 'Masculinity' has been marked by closure throughout its history, holding things in place, symbolised by the unitary sexuality of the penis. 'Femininity' has always challenged this, but in the various voices of contemporary psychoanalytic feminism it has managed to articulate this challenge in an unavoidable form, combining seductiveness with content. This has left masculinity in a void, and men at something of a loss; but the uncertainty which results can produce excitement as well as fear. The instability of subject positions which is a consequence of the various challenges to fixed versions of sexual difference outlined in this book, is something to be welcomed. It makes movement possible, however difficult it may also be; and while we may choose to deal with the anxiety this produces by withdrawing into the fixed positions of the past, we have at least been exposed to the possibility of constant, everlasting change.

References

Adams, P. (1989) 'Of Female Bondage'. In T. Brennan (ed) *Between Feminism and Psychoanalysis* London: Routledge.

Anzieu, D. (1975) *Freud's Self-Analysis* London: Hogarth Press, 1986.

Bakan, D. (1958) *Sigmund Freud and the Jewish Mystical Tradition* London: Free Association Books, 1990.

Banton, R., Clifford, P., Frosh, S., Lousada, J. and Rosenthall, J. (1985) *The Politics of Mental Health* London: Macmillan.

Benjamin, J. (1988) *The Bonds of Love* London: Virago, 1990.

Benvenuto, B. and Kennedy, R. (1986) *Introduction to the Work of Jacques Lacan* London: Free Association Books.

Berman, M. (1982) *All That is Solid Melts into Air* London: Verso, 1983.

Bernheimer, C. and Kahane, C. (1985) *In Dora's Case* London: Virago.

Bion, W. (1962) *Learning from Experience* London: Maresfield.

Bly, R. (1990) *Iron John* Brisbane: Element.

Bowie, M. (1991) *Lacan* London: Fontana.

Braidotti, R. (1989) 'The Politics of Ontological Difference'. In T. Brennan (ed) *Between Feminism and Psychoanalysis* London: Routledge.

Brennan, T. (1989) (ed) *Between Feminism and Psychoanalysis* London: Routledge.

Breuer, J. and Freud, S. (1895) *Studies in Hysteria* Harmondsworth: Penguin, 1974.

Brittan, A. (1989) *Masculinity and Power* Oxford: Blackwell.

Chasseguet-Smirgel, J. (1975) *The Ego Ideal* London: Free Association Books, 1985.

Cixous, H. (1975) Sorties. In E. Marks and I. de Courtivon (eds) *New French Feminisms* Sussex: Harvester, 1981.

Cixous, H. (1976) The Laugh of the Medusa. In E. Marks and I. de Courtivon (eds) *New French Feminisms* Sussex: Harvester, 1981.

Clément, C. (1983) *The Lives and Legends of Jacques Lacan* New York: Columbia University Press.

Diller, J. (1991) *Freud's Jewish Identity: A Case Study in the Impact of Ethnicity* London: Associated University Presses.

Dyer, R. (1982) 'Don't Look Now – The Male Pin-up'. *Screen 23*, 3–4.

Eichenbaum, L. and Orbach, S. (1982) *Outside In . . . Inside Out* Harmondsworth: Penguin.

Elliott, A. (1992) *Social Theory and Psychoanalysis in Transition* Oxford: Blackwell.

Felman, S. (1987) *Jacques Lacan and the Adventure of Insight* Cambridge, Mass.: Harvard University Press.

Finkelhor, D. (1984) *Child Sexual Abuse* New York: Free Press.

Fogel, G. (1986) *The Psychology of Men* New York: Basic Books.

Forrester, J. (1987) 'The Seminars of Jacques Lacan: In Place of an Introduction. Book 1: Freud's Papers on Technique, 1953–1954'. *Free Associations 10*, 63–93.

Freud, S. (1900) *The Interpretation of Dreams* Harmondsworth: Penguin, 1976.

Freud, S. (1905) Fragment of an Analysis of a Case of Hysteria. In S. Freud, *Case Histories* Harmondsworth: Penguin, 1977.

Freud, S. (1913) The Theme of the Three Caskets. In S. Freud, *Art and Literature* Harmondsworth: Penguin, 1985.

Freud, S. (1925a) Some Psychical Consequences of the Anatomical Distinction Between the Sexes. In S. Freud, *On Sexuality* Harmondsworth: Penguin, 1977.

Freud, S. (1925b) Negation. In S. Freud, *On Metapsychology* Harmondsworth: Penguin, 1984.

Freud, S. (1933) *New Introductory Lectures on Psychoanalysis* Harmondsworth: Penguin, 1973.

Freud, S. (1937) *Analysis Terminable and Interminable* London: Hogarth Press.

Freud, S. (1939) Moses and Monotheism. In S. Freud, *The Origins of Religion* Harmondsworth: Penguin, 1985.

Frosh, S. (1987a) *The Politics of Psychoanalysis* London: Macmillan.

Frosh, S. (1987b) 'Issues for Men Working with Sexually Abused Children'. *British Journal of Psychotherapy 3*, 332–9.

Frosh, S. (1988) 'No Man's Land? The Role of Men Working with Sexually Abused Children'. *British Journal of Guidance and Counselling 16*, 1–10.

Frosh, S. (1989) *Psychoanalysis and Psychology* London: Macmillan.

Frosh, S. (1991) *Identity Crisis: Modernity, Psychoanalysis and the Self* London: Macmillan.

Frosh, S. (1992a) Masculine Ideology and Psychological Therapy. In J. Ussher and P. Nicolson (eds) *Gender Issues in Clinical Psychology* London: Routledge.

Frosh, S. (1992b) Response to Gellner. In W. Dryden and C. Feltham (eds) *Psychotherapy and its Discontents* Buckingham: Open University Press.

Gallop, J. (1982) *Feminism and Psychoanalysis* London: Macmillan.

Gallop, J. (1988) *Thinking Through the Body* New York: Columbia University Press.

Gellner, E. (1992) Psychoanalysis, Social Role and Testability. In W. Dryden and C. Feltham (eds) *Psychotherapy and its Discontents* Buckingham: Open University Press.

Glaser, D. and Frosh, S. (1988) *Child Sexual Abuse* London: Macmillan.

Glaser, D. and Frosh, S. (1993) *Child Sexual Abuse (Second Edition)* London: Macmillan.

Grosz, E. (1990) *Jacques Lacan: A Feminist Introduction* London: Routledge.

Grosz, E. (1992) Kristeva, Julia. In E. Wright (ed) *Feminism and Psychoanalysis: A Critical Dictionary* Oxford: Blackwell.

Grunberger, B. (1979) *Narcissism: Psychoanalytic Essays* New York: International Universities Press.

Grunberger, B. (1989) *New Essays on Narcissism* London: Free Association Books.

Haugaard, J. and Reppucci, N. (1988) *The Sexual Abuse of Children* San Francisco: Jossey-Bass.

Heath, S. (1987) Male Feminism. In A. Jardine and P. Smith (eds) *Men in Feminism* London: Methuen.

Hinshelwood, R. (1989) *A Dictionary of Kleinian Thought* London: Free Association Books.

Hollway, W. (1989) *Subjectivity and Method in Psychology* London: Sage.

Irigaray, L. (1977) *This Sex Which is Not One* Ithaca: Cornell University Press, 1985.

Irigaray, L. (1989) The Gesture in Psychoanalysis. In T. Brennan (ed) *Between Feminism and Psychoanalysis* London: Routledge.

Jacobus, M. (1986) 'Madonna: Like a Virgin'. *Oxford Literary Review 8*, 35–50.
Jacobus, M. (1990) ' "Tea Daddy": Poor Mrs. Klein and the Pencil Shavings'. *Women 1*, 160–79.
Jones, E. (1955) *Sigmund Freud: Life and Work* London: Hogarth Press.
Kristeva, J. (1979) Women's Time. In T. Moi (ed) *The Kristeva Reader* Oxford: Blackwell.
Kristeva, J. (1980) *Powers of Horror* New York: Columbia University Press, 1982.
Kristeva, J. (1983) Freud and Love. In T. Moi (ed) *The Kristeva Reader* Oxford: Blackwell.
Kristeva, J. (1987) *Black Sun* New York: Columbia University Press, 1989.
Lacan, J. (1953) The Function and Field of Speech and Language in Psychoanalysis. In J. Lacan *Écrits: A Selection* London: Tavistock, 1977.
Lacan, J. (1953–4) *The Seminars of Jacques Lacan, Book I* Cambridge: Cambridge University Press, 1988.
Lacan, J. (1954–5) *The Seminars of Jacques Lacan, Book II* Cambridge: Cambridge University Press, 1988.
Lacan, J. (1957) The Agency of the Letter in the Unconscious of Reason Since Freud. In J. Lacan *Écrits: A Selection* London: Tavistock, 1977.
Lacan, J. (1958) The Meaning of the Phallus. In J. Mitchell and J. Rose (eds) *Feminine Sexuality* London: Macmillan, 1982.
Lacan, J. (1964) Guiding Remarks for a Congress on Feminine Sexuality. In J. Mitchell and J. Rose (eds) *Feminine Sexuality* London: Macmillan, 1982.
Lacan, J. (1972–3) Seminar XX: Encore. In J. Mitchell and J. Rose (eds) *Feminine Sexuality* London: Macmillan, 1982.
Laplanche, J. and Leclaire, S. (1966) 'The Unconscious'. *Yale French Studies 48*, 118–75 (1972).
Levidow, L. (1989) Witches and Seducers: Moral Panics for Our Time. In B. Richards (ed) *Crises of the Self* London: Free Association Books.
Levinas, E. (1947) Time and the Other. In S. Hand (ed) *The Levinas Reader* Oxford: Blackwell, 1989.
Lyotard, J.-F. (1979) *The Postmodern Condition* Manchester: Manchester University Press, 1984.
MacLeod, M. and Sarraga, E. (1988) 'Challenging the Orthodoxy: Towards a Feminist Theory and Practice'. *Feminist Review 28*, 16–55.
Mann, T. (1933) *Joseph and His Brothers* Harmondsworth: Penguin.
Mitchell, J. (1974) *Psychoanalysis and Feminism* Harmondsworth: Penguin.
Mitchell, J. and Rose, J. (1982) (eds) *Feminine Sexuality* London: Macmillan.
Moi, T. (1985) *Sexual/Textual Politics* London: Methuen.
Moi, T. (1989) Patriarchal Thought and the Drive for Knowledge. In T. Brennan (ed) *Between Feminism and Psychoanalysis* London: Routledge.
Moore, S. (1988) Getting a Bit of the Other: The Pimps of Postmodernism. In R. Chapman and T. Rutherford (eds) *Male Order* London: Lawrence and Wishart.
Olivier, C. (1980) *Jocasta's Children* London: Routledge, 1989.
Ragland-Sullivan, E. (1991) The Sexual Masquerade: A Lacanian Theory of Sexual Difference. In E. Ragland-Sullivan and M. Bracher (eds) *Lacan and the Subject of Language* New York: Routledge.
Resnick, S. (1987) *The Theatre of the Dream* London: Tavistock.
Roith, E. (1987) *The Riddle of Freud* London: Tavistock.
Roudinesco, E. (1986) *Jacques Lacan and Co.* Chicago: University of Chicago Press, 1990.
Rutherford, J. (1988) Who's that Man? In R. Chapman and J. Rutherford (eds) *Male Order* London: Lawrence and Wishart.

Sayers, J. (1991) *Mothering Psychoanalysis* London: Hamish Hamilton.

Segal, H. (1973) *Introduction to the Work of Melanie Klein* London: Hogarth Press.

Segal, L. (1987) *Is the Future Female?* London: Virago.

Segal, L. (1990) *Slow Motion: Changing Men* London: Virago.

Seidler, V. (1985) Fear and Intimacy. In A. Metcalfe and M. Humphries (eds) *The Sexuality of Men* London: Pluto Press.

Seidler, V. (1989) *Rediscovering Masculinity* London: Routledge.

Seidler, V. (1991) *Recreating Sexual Politics* London: Routledge.

Shiach, M. (1989) 'Their "symbolic" exists, it holds power – we the sowers of disorder know it only too well.' In T. Brennan (ed) *Between Feminism and Psychoanalysis* London: Routledge.

Smith, P. (1987) Men in Feminism. In A. Jardine and P. Smith (eds) *Men in Feminism* London: Methuen.

Theweleit, K. (1977) *Male Fantasies* Cambridge: Polity, 1987.

Ussher, J. and Baker, C. (1993) (eds) *Psychological Perspectives on Sexual Problems* London: Routledge.

Ussher, J. and Nicolson, P. (1992) (eds) *Gender Issues in Clinical Psychology* London: Routledge.

Whitford, M. (1989) Rereading Irigaray. In T. Brennan (ed) *Between Feminism and Psychoanalysis* London: Routledge.

Wright, E. (1989) Thoroughly Postmodern Feminist Criticism. In T. Brennan (ed) *Between Feminism and Psychoanalysis* London: Routledge.

Name index

Subject index